# Teens' Guide to Dating

Expert Advice & Tips for Building
Healthy, Happy Relationships &
Everything You Need to Know About
Crushes & Heartbreak

# Contents

# Trigger Warning

This book contains information about how to date in a respectful manner, and as such, deals with issues of consent. Some stories and examples included here mention aspects of sexual assault, internet pornography, grooming, and abusive relationships.

This book also deals with the practical side of sexual relationships. This chapter is clearly labelled, and information is imparted in a non-gratuitous manner. This chapter also includes unbiased information about sexually transmitted diseases, contraception, and abortions.

# Introduction

M ANY PEOPLE START DATING others when they hit their teenage years. It's not compulsory; however, much of the media would like us to think that it is, and if you don't want to—or don't manage to—secure a couple of dates before you hit adulthood, there's no evidence that you'll be scarred and disadvantaged for life. In fact, as reported by Ayer, a study by the University of Georgia indicates that not dating in your teenage years can actually leave you with slightly better social skills than your classmates who did. (Ayer, 2019).

However, if you analyze lots of the books, TV shows, and movies aimed at a teenage audience, you'll see that the theme of dating comes up again and again, even when the main plot is something to do with zombies. There's no getting away from the message that you're supposed to be falling in and out of love on a monthly basis, but the reality of modern teenage romances is actually much different.

Those teens who have started dating tend to be very loud and obvious about it. They will post on social media, tell all their friends about it at school, and publicly display their affection for their partner while out and about. This can make it seem like everyone is loved up when actually it is just a shouty minority. However, if you're not one of them, it can leave you feeling left out or left behind.

I'm going to come clean right now; this book is not going to tell you how to get a date, how to get someone to like you back, or offer you a five-step solution to dating bliss. What it is going to do is:

- show you how to feel confident talking to new people

- help you figure out what kind of relationship you're ready for, or if you're not ready for one at all

- teach you how to enjoy your relationships by setting clear boundaries and always being comfortable

- highlight how important communication is, whether that's telling your partner what you need or listening to their expectations

- give you examples of what healthy, and unhealthy, romantic relationships will look like for teenagers, so that you can make good judgments about your own

- arm you with the information you need to always be safe on dates, online, and when ending a relationship

Why is all that important? Dating isn't just something you should do because you think you're supposed to. It can be a wonderful experience, forming a close relationship with someone else and enjoying the butterflies in your stomach every time they look at you, but you can't force it. By working on your self-confidence first, you will feel more capable of handling different situations and, therefore, getting the best out of the experience.

## The Confidence to Stay Safe

As an inner-city cop, I saw my fair share of domestic disputes, relationship bust-ups, and the results of poor decisions. Too many young people were putting themselves in situations where they weren't safe; some because they didn't know better, but many because they didn't think they were worth better. I wanted to do something about it: to empower the next generation of teenagers to know that they can ask for what they want, say no to what they don't, and have the confidence to put their own safety first in any relationship.

I know when I was a teenager, I barely had the confidence to look in the mirror, let alone gaze into the eyes of an attractive girl. In fact, I'll share a couple of embarrassing dating stories along the way to help you realize that even when things go badly, there's always hope that the next person will laugh with you, rather than at you.

## The Confidence to Step Out of the Shadows

Your teenage years are the time when you're growing into your future self, and you'll be eager to try on all sorts of personas and attitudes to see if they fit. Just like shopping for clothes, some will be too big, some too small, and some will make you feel like a complete fool, but eventually you will find the perfect you. Until then, feeling like things don't quite fit can make you reluctant to get out there, and I go into more detail about this in my book *Teens' Guide to Making Friends*. It's completely normal to feel like you look a little odd or everyone is looking at you; it's all down to the way your brain starts to rewire itself as it prepares you for a more adult way of thinking.

However, you really shouldn't make it through your teens by hiding yourself away. Building social skills, learning from your mistakes, and experimenting with different friendship groups are all important life lessons you need to learn. The benefits of learning them in your teens are that you'll be doing so along with all of your peers, and then you'll have them all ready for when you're an adult. I know it can seem scary doing something like asking your crush out, but it's not going to be any less scary in your twenties or thirties, might as well give it a go now when everyone is feeling a little weird about things.

## The Confidence to Be Independent

All of your relationships go through a seismic shift during puberty. You'll find yourself falling out with old friends, falling in love with new ones, and then quite possibly falling out with them too! Friendships evolve as the people in them change, and you'll start to find those ride or dies who will still have your back when you're walking with a cane and complaining about "kids these days."

You'll also find yourself pulling away from your caregivers and craving the autonomy to make your own decisions and create your own rules. During this time, the relationships with your friends and your romantic partners are incredibly important because they will provide you with the emotional support and intimacy that you used to get from family (Sorensen, 2007). Healthy dating relationships can help teens like you grow in confidence, mature in their ability to deal with rejection and loss, and promote self-discovery.

## The Confidence to Know When It's Right

Dating is not about having any partner; it's about know-ing how to find someone you are attracted to and com-patible with, and most importantly, someone who feels the same way about you. This is going to give you your best chance of having a healthy and fulfilling relationship. If you're desperate for a partner—any partner—I can almost guarantee you're going to end up with the wrong partner.

Think back to all those romance movies. Most of the time the characters weren't even looking for a relationship, but they met someone who found their way into their thoughts and then their heart. Getting relationships right is a mixture of finding the right person and behaving in the right way. I can't help you with the first one, but if you keep reading, you'll find plenty of information about the second.

Oh, and those embarrassing stories I promised? Here's the first one to show you how having the confidence to make the first move might actually get you somewhere, even if it didn't quite work out for me in the end.

Back when I was 13, I didn't have the confidence to ask out the girl I liked, so I roped in my best mate Joe to do it for me. I agonized for days over the perfect note to her, which he duly delivered, and then agonized for a few more after she didn't reply. Honestly, those were the longest two days of my life. So, imagine my surprise when I turn up to class on the third day and there's a note sitting on my desk from my beloved, telling me to meet her at the bus stop after school!

Unfortunately, a lunchtime football game was to ruin our plans, as I ended up with a twisted ankle and had to make an emergency trip to A&E to make sure it wasn't more serious. Thankfully, Joe agreed to go to the bus stop instead and let her know that we'd have to reschedule. Never has time passed more slowly than when I was waiting to be discharged, desperately hoping Joe had managed to sort everything out for me. Of course, it's so much easier now that you all have phones, but back then we didn't have that option.

I was just about to leave when an ambulance pulled up, and out wheeled Joe, his face covered in blood. It turned out my crush's older brother had found out about our intended date and turned up determined to defend his sister's honor. Joe ended up with a broken nose—he never got the chance to explain he was just the messenger—and I was terrified of asking anyone out for a very long time!

## YOUR FREE GIFT

As a token of gratitude for reading this book, I am excited to present you with a gift that will help improve your confidence. Introducing "The Teens' Guide to Overcoming Shyness".

A guide with conversation topics, questions, and tips to help individuals start meaningful and engaging conversations with anyone.

Pick up your free copy here:

# Teens' Guide Series

Teens' Guide to Making Friends

Click

Teens' Guide to Making Friends

Teens' Guide to Health and Mental Wellness

Click

Teens' Guide to Health and Mental Wellness

# Chapter One

---

# How to Love Yourself

*I F YOU DON'T LOVE yourself, how in the world are you going to love somebody else?* –RuPaul

Some teens find it really hard to feel positive about themselves during puberty. Your skin won't behave, hair starts growing wildly, and you can't trust your voice to stay level or your emotions not to flare up. Some days it can feel like you're on a runaway roller coaster and all you want to do is get off, but someone else has the controls. Personally, I hated feeling like I wasn't in control of either my body or my brain. Someone would ask me a perfectly reasonable question, and I'd hear myself rant and rave in response, all the time trying desperately to apply the emergency brakes. This sense of being "wrong" and "broken" was made even worse by watching classmates who seemed much better put together, with flawless complexions, perfect eyebrows, and bodies that actually seemed in proportion.

When you don't look, feel, or act like "you," it can be pretty depressing. Your self-esteem plummets and you start pulling away from social situations in case your inner puberty monster takes the reins again. Back when I was a lad (old person anecdote alert!) we just had to suck it up and get on with things, and if you accidentally yelled at your caregivers, you were in deep trouble. Today a lot more is understood about mental health and the way puberty affects your brain chemistry. This means there is much more good advice out there about dealing with the bad days, and your parents are equipped with better information about how to help.

## Would You Date You?

One huge roadblock that stops a lot of teens from acting on their crushes is the worry that the object of their affections will turn them down, and probably not gently either; teens aren't known for their tact. Why bother even trying when you know that they definitely won't be interested because you can list off the top of your head all the things that are wrong with you? And that right there is exactly the problem: low self-esteem and no self-confidence aren't very attractive qualities.

So, how are you supposed to go about getting a date if you wouldn't date yourself? You need to improve your self-image so that you feel more confident, because—rather than shiny hair or a killer dress sense—confidence really is the most attractive quality you can have.

Think of the confident people in your school. I bet others are drawn to them and want to be their friends. This is because confident people know their own value, and people like to surround themselves with people who have a similar worth—if you're awesome, why would you settle for anyone who isn't? Being accepted into a confident group must mean that they have judged you worthy, so your own opinion of yourself goes up.

Unfortunately, the opposite is also true. Look at the kids at school who are always alone. Do they look confident? Lack of confidence is off-putting—you give off the aura that there's something so bad about you that even you don't want to hang out with yourself. Nobody wants to be around such negative vibes all the time, so they look for friends with more positive outlooks.

## Redesigning Your Self-Image

You can't inflate your self-confidence overnight, but there are a few things you can do to start improving it. It sounds obvious, but if you know that you look good, you'll feel more confident, so pepping up your outside is the easiest way to make you feel better on the inside.

- Why not try a new hairstyle? At the very least, give it a trim and a tidy-up. Also, make sure you're washing it frequently. The same hormones that make your face feel oily can also make your hair more greasy, so aim for a shampoo at least every other day. If you menstruate, you might find that your hair is greasier toward the end of your cycle, so you should wash it more frequently. You could also find some online tutorials for some stylish ways to put your hair up that are much more interesting than just pulling it into a ponytail or a bun.

- Invest in good skincare. Unfortunately, how badly you suffer from acne is genetic, so if you've seen old pictures of pimply relatives, you're probably in for the same bad luck. But the effects of acne can be minimized by keeping your skin clean and preventing dirt from building up in your pores. A gentle cleanser and moisturizer, used daily, can keep breakouts under control. And for the really bad days, there's always concealer to take away some of the redness.

- Treat yourself to a few new clothes that really suit you. It doesn't have to be an entire wardrobe, but having one or two outfits that you know fit well and make you look great can make all the difference. Do you know someone with a creative touch? Maybe they can help you customize some old clothes with patches, embroidery, or other finishing touches. A new outfit needn't be expensive either; plenty of thrift stores have vintage clothes that are coming back into fashion—you never know what bargains you will find!

## A Little Self-Love Goes a Long Way

Knowing you look good on the outside can give you a temporary boost, but if you want to develop true confidence, you need to really believe in yourself. There are so many changes happening to you right now that feel negative; it can be hard to find the positives. But it's really important during these disruptive years to be kind to yourself and show the emerging you some love.

## Be Your Own Cheerleader

Make an effort to celebrate every success or achievement, no matter how small. If you feel like hiding in bed all day, but you manage to get up and dress, you deserve a round of applause! Every time you make a choice that is healthy, for your mind or your body, make sure you acknowledge the win. Chose an apple instead of a cookie? Win! Went for a walk instead of scrolling through socials? Win! Finished your homework on time, tidied your room, and still had time to video chat with your bestie? Win, win, win!

You might be a little too old for stickers and reward charts now, but the visual representation of your achievements is still powerful. Why don't you collect a bunch of jellybeans or M&Ms and drop them into a jar when you have a win? Start with a small one and you'll be surprised how quickly you can fill it—and once it's full, you can take it to the movies for some enjoyment!

Other options are:

- Add pen or sticker dots to a calendar so you can see how many times you succeeded each day.

- Add paper clips to a chain hanging from your wall and watch it grow with your confidence.

- Keep a stash of fake flowers and add one to a vase to acknowledge a positive choice. You'll soon build a beautiful bunch over the week.

## Collect Positivity

If you want to focus on the positives, you need to know what they are. Start looking for things you like about yourself. It might feel hard, and finding the negatives is always so much easier, but I promise you, there will definitely be some good things. Do you always look out for your friends? Are you happy to care for younger siblings? Maybe you really like the shape of your knees.

It's easier to feel good about yourself if you know that other people believe in you too. Try asking friends and family members what they think your best qualities are. It's always easier to see the good points in others than to see your own. I bet you could list five amazing things about each of your friends without missing a beat, and they'll be able to do the same for you. Write them down in a journal so you can remind yourself when you're having a bad day.

Once you've collected a few positive thoughts, you need to find ways to focus on them. I know it sounds stupid, but try starting your day by saying nice things to your reflection. By taking the time to recognize your good points, you start to change the way you think about yourself, with the emphasis being drawn away from negative thoughts and toward a more positive opinion. And, if you feel daft starting every day by telling yourself, "You have great knees and always look good in shorts," you can try some of the following general affirmations instead:

- I deserve to have a good day today.

- Just because someone doesn't see my worth, doesn't mean I have none.

- It's okay to not be perfect.

- Every problem I face today can be solved.

- My flaws and my mistakes are part of me, and I am beautiful.

- I can choose what I do, how I feel, and how I react.

- I am allowed to feel happy and positive about myself and my choices.

## How to Grow Your Confidence

We've dealt with how you look and how you feel inside; next on the list for a positivity makeover is how you act. Confidence fills you up: You have better posture, stand taller, smile more, and are happy making eye contact with others. If you lack confidence, you can end up resembling a deflating balloon: slouching, being aware of your own deficiencies, and being shoved to the back of the pack.

## Use Your Body Language

Your body language says much more about you than the words you use. Ever had a friend tell you they're fine, but you could tell they're not because of the way they stood, their tone of voice, and the tears welling in their eyes? Body language is often communicated unconsciously, meaning you don't choose how your body reacts, making it a more trustworthy indicator of how someone feels.

Still, there are ways to cheat the system. Some well-known body language cues like blushing or sweating are difficult to fake—unless you're a sociopath or a movie star—but others are a piece of cake.

To appear confident:

- make eye contact with the person you're talking to

- keep your back straight and your shoulders open

- avoid fidgeting with your hands or shuffling your feet

Try practicing some of these in the mirror. You should be able to see the difference between your normal posture and a more confident pose. If you're not sure what to aim for, try looking online for some videos of public figures, or watch some TED talk intros.

## A Little More Conversation

If one of the things that make you shy away from social situations is the conversation, you're not alone. Even adults hate the thought that someone might approach us and start a conversation, especially if it's a time we're not expecting it, like in an elevator, at the doctor's office, or queuing for the bathroom.

However, when you're on a date, you kinda have to talk to the other person, otherwise it's going to get very awkward very quickly. So, before you put yourself in that situation, you can use other daily situations to practice some easy conversation starters. It's pretty likely that you have plenty of opportunities during the weekday to talk to other teens. Even if you're home-schooled and your only classmate is the dog, there will be teens somewhere in your neighborhood; you just might have to do a little hunting.

The best way to start a casual conversation is to choose a topic that you know you will both have something to say about. In school, this might be:

- a common subject

- the class you've just finished or are about to start

- a school sports team's performance

- opinions on teachers (try to keep it civil!)

- a question about homework

TEENS' GUIDE TO DATING

- complaints about the cafeteria food

They might not be the most thrilling conversation topics, but they can help you practice conversation because the replies you get are likely to be predictable. Why is this helpful? You can script an opening remark easily, but trying to predict the rest of the conversation won't necessarily go as smoothly. But with topics like these, you'll already have a good idea of what the other person will say, so you can think of a few follow-up remarks in advance.

Here's a good example:

*Hey, what did you think of that chemistry test last week?*

How many possible responses are there? They're either going to say it was easy or hard, they hated it, or that it wasn't too bad. What do you do next? Either agree or disagree. Maybe single out a specific question that you weren't sure about and ask if they knew it. You could even start complaining about the teacher setting too many quizzes. Once you get into a conversation with a familiar subject, it's easy to find things to say.

Another thing to think about is where you're going to try and strike up your conversation. Once again, I wouldn't recommend the bathroom. It's not a place for chatting, even if the acoustics are pretty good. If you have time between classes where you find yourself waiting with others, that's a perfect opportunity. You're all in the same place, about to start the same class—or having just finished it—so you have a common topic and a limited amount of time. Why is that important? If you want to keep the conversation brief and make sure you can get out of it before you start to falter, having something happening soon, like another class or a bus ride, is a great get-out clause. On the flip side, if they're enjoying your company, they might want to keep talking, and you never know, you might even end up sitting together, becoming friends, or even more.

## Learn to Show Your Best Self

You've had your hair cut, put on your best outfit, and spent a few weeks getting through small talk with your peers without turning into a blushing, stammering wreck. It's time to try your newfound confidence out in the real world. Maybe you have a school dance, a birthday party, or a club social coming up that you've been working toward. Or maybe there's a special person you have been getting up the courage to talk to. Either way, there are just a few steps left to take to make sure you can handle yourself in any situation.

I've already shown how you feel more confident if you know that you look good, but you also feel more confident if you are comfortable. In fact, confidence and comfort go hand in hand, and it's difficult to have one without the other. Imagine you had to take a test: Would you feel more confident taking it in the school hall with everyone watching, or alone in your bedroom? I'd bet anything you chose the second option.

While you're growing your confidence, it's perfectly okay to want to stick to places inside your comfort zone. Meet new people on your terms; somewhere you are happy and comfortable: the mall, a favorite shop, the skate park, the library, a regular club, or your school. An added bonus of this is that the other people you meet will be comfortable there too, so you instantly have something in common. If you take yourself to a party where you feel completely out of your depth, the chances are that you and the people you meet there aren't going to have much common ground.

## Finding Comfort in the Unknown

Stepping out of your comfort zone doesn't have to mean throwing yourself into the deep end. Those big social events I mentioned earlier? Chances are they're not part of your normal stomping ground. If you want to try something new, that's fantastic. New experiences can be so much fun, and there are ways to minimize the discomfort.

- Go with a group of friends. They will be familiar

and predictable, and you will still feel comfortable in their company, even if you're all in a new social situation.

- Stick to comfortable activities. If dancing isn't your forté, hang out at the side or find some tables to sit at.

- Find out what kind of things will be happening throughout the night so nothing catches you off guard. Ask people who have been before what to expect.

- Decide on a leaving time and stick to it. You will feel more in control if you know how the night will end.

- Have somewhere quiet you can go if you need a break. The bathroom, the garden, the car, or just a corner of the room away from the main activity.

- Visit the venue beforehand if possible so you know where everything is. Just knowing that you can find the bathroom without getting flustered can be extremely reassuring.

## Stay True to Yourself

None of the advice in this chapter is asking you to change anything fundamental about yourself. Rather, it is designed to help you feel comfortable in your own skin and highlight your best features. Sometimes people feel that a radical change is needed in order to bring them some confidence, so a different haircut or trying a new style of clothing feels exciting. Others know what they like and find comfort in just putting out the most polished version of that. The most important thing is to find reasons to love yourself so that you grow more confident sending that person out into the world.

# Chapter Two

## Am I Ready to Date?

*IT'S NICE TO HAVE a crush on someone. It feels like you're alive, you know?* –Scarlett Johansson

I don't know, are you? There isn't a test you need to take or a set of achievements you need to fulfill first. At the end of the day, only you can answer this question. A more important one to consider would be: Why are you asking?

Movies, TV shows, and books will tell you that dating is an important part of being a teenager. In fact, it seems as if the minute any character hits puberty, all their motivations and desires switch to a single focus: finding "the one." From Bella literally giving up life to be with Edward, Lara Jean considering throwing away her shot at her dream college to be with Peter, to studious Tessa taking on all of Hardin's problems; it seems like all your favorite characters are chasing love in some form or another.

It's true that society as a whole seems to place an awful lot of importance on romantic relationships. Married couples even get more benefits and better legal protection than single people or those in committed but not legally defined unions. But all of this constant pressure to find someone to couple up with can lead to a lot of issues, especially when the goal of being part of a couple becomes more important than who the other person actually is.

Even if you do find someone you're attracted to, the thought of taking the next step can be scary. What if they don't feel the same way? If you do start dating, what will they expect from you? If you've never been in a romantic relationship before, and the only reference points you have are the idyllic sweeping romances of Hollywood, it's no wonder you can feel a little out of your depth.

Asking someone out can be a big step, and not everyone wants to act on these feelings. Just because your hormones and your brain chemicals have decided that they like a person, doesn't mean you have to act on it if you aren't ready. Many teens have social, religious, and cultural reasons for not dating, but that doesn't mean they aren't attracted to others. Ultimately, while you might find yourself attracted to someone, if you're not ready to handle an intense and intimate relationship, you might not find dating a positive experience.

## Different Experiences

It might seem obvious, but I'm going to state it anyway: Dating at 13 will look vastly different than dating at 18. Not only in terms of the sexual activities involved but also in how emotionally mature you are. I'm not going to tell you that a pair of 13-year-olds can't fall in love—they absolutely can and it will be real and intense and all-consuming—but that love will look and feel different than love at 16, 18, 25, and so on.

Early relationships are supposed to be exciting and fun, full of sneaky glances across the classroom, stolen kisses in the stairwell, and happy memories of dates with an early curfew. They don't need to be soured or complicated by trying to grow up too fast or introduce more mature experiences that you aren't physically or emotionally ready for.

Older teenage relationships are more complex; you'll be able to support each other, become more intimately involved by the sharing of problems, worries, and secrets, and start adding more physical elements. While bringing you closer together, increasing the intensity of your feelings for each other, and still being wonderful fun, these relationships also require additional responsibilities. Always make sure you know what the age of consent is in your country or state, and remember that there can be real consequences for crossing it, so always be well informed. Look after each other, be safe, and never do anything you are uncomfortable with.

When talking about relationships in this book, I'm going to try and address all the different types and experiences that people will have. Whether your first date is at 13 or 19, the advice given here will still apply. However, I have also included a number of illustrative examples to show you some real relationships in action and some of the kinds of situations you might find yourself in. Some of these examples will contain activities and experiences aimed at younger teens, and some at older teens, and they are by no means meant to tell you that your relationship must have all of those elements. I think it is important for teens of all ages to be aware of some situations that might occur, even if it will be many years in the future, so that they can be adequately prepared to deal with them, and I have tried my best to indicate those examples that are aimed at older teenagers by including the ages of those involved.

## Defining Relationships

The term "relationship" is most commonly used to mean a romantic one, but actually, it is just a way to describe how people know each other. You have relationships with your family members, teachers, friends, and even the school bus driver. While most of these are platonic, many of them involve love, intimacy, and commitment—qualities that society has taught us are usually reserved for partners only. In fact, for many people, some of these relationships are more fulfilling and more important than romantic relationships.

Everyone needs a mixture of different relationships in their lives because each one has a different function and teaches you something different. Relationships mutate and evolve overtime, so the best friend you have at five probably won't be the best friend you have as an adult—and you grow closer, too, or further apart from people as you grow up. This can make friendships with your peers the most volatile, as you're both going through rapid changes, whereas relationships you have with adults tend to be more stable.

## Family Bonds

These are the first relationships you ever formed and they can have a huge impact on any other relationships you have during your life. These relationships often have a deep level of connection and intimacy, meaning you feel comfortable together, trust each other, and are able to share and talk about subjects that are important to you.

Once you reach your teenage years, these family bonds are heavily tested because the nature of them shifts. You are striving for more independence and want to be seen on an equal footing with the adults, but they might not be ready for that yet. While things can feel difficult for a few years, these relationships rarely break down completely, instead forming the basis for new friendships where you're both adults.

## Friendships

These change as you grow as well, with younger friendships being more superficial. You're drawn together by your mutual love of dinosaurs or hatred of older siblings. Whereas teenage friendships are deeper and more intense. You will form connections quickly, wanting to spend all your time with these wonderful new humans who truly get you and understand everything you're going through. Friends take over from family as your primary support network, secret keepers, and fonts of knowledge.

## Mentor/Pupil

These relationships occur between any adult and child where there is an exchange of knowledge and a duty of care. Think Obi-Wan and Luke Skywalker, Dumbledore and Harry Potter, or Iron Man and Spider-man. There's a level of respect from your side because you understand that these adults care for you and want you to do well, so you listen to their advice and let them guide you. School teachers, coaches, religious leaders, club leaders; even neighbors, friends' parents, and extended family members can take on these roles in your life.

## Other Relationships

There are other relationships you will have with people in your life who you see less frequently, who aren't interested in developing closer ties with you, or who simply perform a function. These superficial connections never develop any intimacy or depth, but you are still civil and respectful toward each other. You probably won't be pouring your heart out to the mailman, but that doesn't mean you aren't connected.

## What Makes a Romantic Relationship Different?

The majority of healthy relationships you have in your life are platonic: based either on friendship between two people of equal standing, or on mutual respect between you and an adult. Until your teenage years, these are the only two options available to you and they are all that you need to feel happy and socially fulfilled.

Once you enter your teenage years, you unlock a third option: romantic relationships. These feel more intense than friendships; you want to spend all your time together and tell each other everything, and when you're not together, or if you've had a fight, it can feel physically painful. However, it's important to note that this stage of intense attraction and infatuation doesn't last. Once it burns out, many romantic relationships falter as you start to notice each other's differences and annoying traits.

## Just Friends... or More?

Most people would define a romantic relationship by its physical side—hugging, kissing, holding hands, sexual contact—but this is a very short-sighted view. Lots of friends hug and hold hands, and air kissing is a common greeting for friends and family in many cultures. On the other side, there are also good reasons why romantic relationships wouldn't involve physical contact, including religious, cultural, and personal preferences.

A better marker for a romantic relationship might be feelings of attraction toward the other person. We often think of attraction as being purely physical, but it actually has a lot of different components. The more you get to know someone, the more likely you are to feel attracted to them, which makes sense because closer relationships involve more intimacy anyway, so you feel a deeper connection. This is why people who have been friends for years can find themselves developing romantic attraction, even though their physical appearances haven't changed.

Other factors that can cause you to feel attracted to someone are: how comfortable you feel around each other, how similar your interests and values are, and how likely they are to reciprocate your feelings (BBC Bitesize, 2019). As you get older, you'll become more sure about what you like, and the kind of people you become attracted to will change, but as a teenager or a young adult, part of the dating experience is trying new things and finding out what works for you.

## Exceptions to The Rules

Society's opinions, expectations, and stereotypes continue to be shockingly heteronormative, despite the fact that we no longer live in that world. This view of romantic relationships doesn't take into account the feelings and actions of an increasingly large minority of people who don't identify as cishet.

Aromantics don't feel romantic attraction toward others, but they can still crave the intimacy of a close relationship.

Whereas asexuals don't feel sexual attraction toward others, but they still feel romantic desires and enjoy many aspects of a romantic relationship.

Some non-binary or trans teens may feel uncomfortable expressing themselves through physical touch, especially if the way their bodies react causes an episode of body dysphoria, while others will still want sex to be part of their relationships.

As much as we would like there to be a clear-cut definition of a romantic relationship, the reality is that everyone's expectations and experiences will be different. Make sure that yours is authentic to your own desires and needs, and not warped into what you think other people want to see.

## They're Doing it; Why Aren't You?

Relationships should grow from shared interests, experiences, philosophies, and attitudes. Each one is unique in the way that it works and what the participants get out of it. You can't decide what relationship you want and then expect to be able to pick a person to tick all of the boxes exactly. Dating should be like browsing Netflix:

You scroll through the available options until you find one that you like, then you spend an enjoyable evening together, preferably with snacks. If you decide you only want to watch a comedy starring Zac Efron, a homicidal cat, and a talking head, you're going to be disappointed by every suggestion that comes up that doesn't have those features. You'll end up trawling through all the streaming and movie rental services in search of a movie that, in the end, might not actually exist.

Think for a minute about your motivations for being interested in dating. Have you met someone you would like to get to know more intimately? Are your friends in relationships or are you feeling left out? Or do you think that dating is normal; therefore, you should be doing it? Let's consider each scenario individually.

## Meeting Someone Special

Lightning strikes! Your stomach turns to butterflies! Everything before this moment was black and white and now your life is in technicolor! In reality, attraction rarely happens in an instant; rather, it grows from a number of sources. It can even take a while for you to realize that you are developing romantic feelings toward someone. Whether you'd even thought about dating before or not, this person has now made you want to grow your relationship in a new direction.

## Feeling Left Out

It can be hard when some friends in your group start dating because they will now be splitting their time between their friends and their partner. Where you and your best friend might have had regular social arrangements—Friday night movies or Saturday at the mall—you're now left alone with nothing to replace them. It can be even worse if several friends date in groups and you're the only single one left. It can be really tempting to look for a romantic relationship to fill the void, or to join in with group dates, but if you're not with the right person or you're not ready for a different type of relationship, you won't be happy.

## Craving Normal

Peer pressure has always been a huge issue for teenagers. When you go through puberty, your brain starts to rewire itself and new connections are made between previously isolated areas. This leads to a new level of self-awareness, and the sense of feeling apart from the "normal" crowd is something that most teenagers feel at some point. When you feel different, the urge to conform and fit in can be overpowering, and this means many teens try to change their behavior or their look—or at least pretend to—in order to copy what everyone else is doing.

The problem is that, often, what you think everyone is getting up to is quite a long way from the truth. If everyone is faking it to fit in, then the actual number of teens you know who are telling the truth about their dating history is probably much lower. You may even find that by being honest and open about your own experiences (or lack thereof), you inspire others to feel more comfortable about theirs.

## Person-Led or Activity-Led?

In the first option, your decision to date is led by existing feelings toward a specific person, but in the other two examples, you're placing more value on the activity itself than on who you're doing it with. Think about it in the context of your other relationships: You became friends with people because you enjoy each other's company, and this means that you have fun together and find the experience rewarding. If you forced yourself to spend time with people you had no interest in, just because it was better than being alone at home, would you enjoy yourself as much? I'm sure you've been to family gatherings where you've felt just like that, so you know how different it feels from hanging out with your friends. Dating the right person can feel completely different from dating the wrong person, or dating half-heartedly because you feel you should.

By the way, that movie does exist, but it stars Ryan Reynolds; close enough though, right?

## Is This Love?

Unsurprisingly, there are also different forms of love, and you've hopefully experienced a couple of them already. The love you have for your caregivers feels different from the love you have for your siblings, your friends, and your pets. Psychologists and scientists have tried to demystify all your emotions and decided that love is made up of three different components: intimacy, commitment, and passion (Myers, 2022). Different types of love utilize different combinations of components. For example, platonic love (between family members or best friends) is a blend of intimacy and commitment, while romantic love is a mixture of intimacy and passion. The ultimate loving relationship should involve a healthy dose of all three.

You can also break love down into the chemicals that are produced by your brain, but this isn't a very sexy definition. There are lots of other things in life that produce large amounts of dopamine—the happy hormone that makes you crave more of whatever released it—such as eating ice cream, completing a good workout, and going on a shopping spree, but spending time with someone you love is very high on the list. The problem with dopamine is that you eventually need more and more of it to get the same high. So, when you stop feeling that burning desire to spend time with your partner, you might feel like the relationship is over. You're left with intimacy without passion or commitment, which is now just friendship.

How do you know when you're really in love with someone? I'm afraid it's not when you dream about them every night, or when you can't keep your hands off each other, or when the very sight of them makes your heart flutter and your knees buckle. That's still the dopamine talking. Love is a combination of intimacy (feeling emotionally close and connected), passion (physical attraction and sexual contact), and commitment (the decision to stay together and maintain your relationship). Out of all three aspects of love, only passion is a passive component, meaning you aren't in control of whether it is there or not, which is why trying to date someone you don't fancy rarely works out well.

## No Substitutes

Because different relationships have these different core aspects, each one fulfills different emotional needs. But—and not everyone realizes this—so many people try and overcompensate for deficient relationships with other types. But that's like trying to fit a square peg into a round hole. A damaged family relationship (intimacy plus commitment) cannot be replaced with a romantic relationship that is lacking commitment and is likely to burn out quickly.

## The Important Ingredients for a Healthy Dating Relationship

Because dating relationships are an entirely new experience, it can be difficult to know what to expect. Yes, we tend to see the wonderful side of things from TV, film, and books, but that doesn't help when you're venturing out on your first forays into the world of romance. You don't have to go to the movies or a funfair for your first date, and it isn't compulsory to give your friends a minute-by-minute account of events the next day, and just because he opens the door for you doesn't mean he is the perfect gentleman.

A healthy relationship is much more than a string of lovely dates and romantic gestures. Rather, it relies on a number of core qualities. These qualities are absolutely essential, and if something is missing, it should be a red flag that you're on course for an unhappy ending.

You know you're in a healthy relationship if:

- you can both communicate honestly about what you feel, want, and need. This lets you find compromises and draw boundaries.

- you feel listened to, and you also listen to your partner. There's no point communicating your needs if they fall on deaf ears.

- you both respect each other and each other's beliefs and values. Nobody should be trying to make you feel uncomfortable or get you to do something you don't want.

- you enjoy spending time together and are interested in each other's achievements. If your partner's company doesn't make you feel happy, there's probably a lack of respect on their part.

- you support each other. If they come to watch your team play, or sit through a horror movie marathon despite hating the sight of blood, they're showing support for your interests.

- you are affectionate toward each other. Physical or verbal affection helps us feel wanted and increases feelings of intimacy, as long as it stays within the boundaries you set.

# Chapter Three

---

## Know Your Boundaries

*I* *F IT'S NOT MAKING you better, it isn't love. True love makes you more of who you are, not less.* –Mandy Hale

All relationships have rules and boundaries that govern how you behave within them. Some of these are consciously set, whereas others seem to have evolved without you even thinking about them. There are things we know we can do—or cannot do—because they will make the other person uncomfortable. For example, I could never swear around my parents, even now as an adult. Heaven forbid, I stubbed my toe or dropped a glass while they were in the room because I couldn't get away with anything worse than "Oh sugar." That's one of the boundaries of our relationship that has been dictated by my parents, and it's important that I respect their wishes and stick to them.

You'll have similar boundaries with your caregivers, and your friends too. They're often easy to set with people you feel close to, like telling a particularly huggy friend that you'd rather not be squeezed at every opportunity. This is one of the benefits of intimacy between you and your friends; you can tell each other your preferences and know that they won't be upset by them... as long as they are reasonable. Yet, setting boundaries in a romantic relationship can sometimes feel like you're denying or restricting your partner, especially if you're the one who wants to move slower. However, the consequences of not speaking up for yourself means that you will very quickly feel out of control and as if your feelings don't matter.

## The Right Kind of Limits

If you're thinking that boundaries sound like limits, you're right, but if you think that limits are a bad thing, then you're only seeing half of the picture. You've had limits put on you since you were a baby; things like, don't drink out of the toilet or don't speak to strangers. These boundaries are designed to keep you safe. As you grow up, some of the other limits you have to deal with can feel more stifling, like having a curfew or not being allowed to go out on a school night. There's also a third kind of limit: when you build a barrier between your true feelings and those that you are happy sharing with others.

So, what's the difference? And how do you recognize whether your relationship is built with the right kind of boundaries? It's all due to who these limits benefit.

- Healthy boundaries let you both set out your expectations for the relationship. They can include things like how often you expect to be in contact, who you tell about your relationship, and how much physical and sexual contact you're comfortable with. These boundaries are based on respect and communication, and by talking about them, you make sure that no one gets upset by expecting something unreasonable.

- Unhealthy limits benefit one partner and disadvantage another. They are often one-sided, with the person imposing the limits and not having to follow them. These are a sign of a co-dependency or a toxic relationship. They can include not letting you spend time with other friends, letting your partner read your phone messages but not allowing you to read theirs, and one person dictating what the other wears.

- Walls and barriers within relationships can make it difficult to really get to know each other properly. Some people want to hide secrets because they are worried that others will think badly of them if they find out, or they may have been hurt before and think that by not letting their partner get too close, they will avoid this happening again.

Have a read through the following relationship problems and see if you can tell which could be solved by communicating boundaries and which has unhealthy boundaries. Would you know what to do in each situation?

## Communication

1. Chantal and Tim have been dating for five weeks. She loves to text him during the day to send him cute pictures, ask him what he's up to, and share funny social media posts. But Tim only replies with emojis or short answers, and he rarely texts her first. When they hang out in person, he's really chatty, always holds her hand, and shows her videos that made him laugh. Chantal is beginning to worry that she's doing something wrong, or that Tim doesn't fancy her anymore.

2. Enrique and Joe have been together for six months and see each other every day. When they're not together, Joe always texts Enrique to see what he's doing, and if he doesn't reply

straight away, Joe will call him. Last week, Enrique's phone fell out of his pocket in the car after soccer practice and Joe couldn't get hold of him for an hour. When he realized it, Enrique went back for it and found 30 missed calls and some very angry voicemails and texts from Joe accusing him of cheating on him.

In both examples, half of each couple expects a lot more communication than the other. Chantal and Tim need to discuss their expectations because it sounds like Chantal wants their texts to be like an ongoing conversation, whereas Tim might feel that they don't need to be in touch as much between dates. However, the relationship between Enrique and Joe is more concerning. Joe expects to know exactly where Enrique is—all of the time. It doesn't sound like he trusts his partner, whereas Enrique feels like he is constantly under supervision and tries not to go places or see people that Joe doesn't approve of. Joe is trying to control Enrique, and this is not a healthy relationship.

## Physical

1. Brad and Yasmin met at a party, had too much to drink, and ended up having sex in the bathroom. Afterward, Yasmin texted Brad to say she had a great time and asked him out on a proper

date. They went to the movies and Yasmin kept stroking his thigh during the film. Afterward, she suggested they pull up somewhere and have sex in Brad's car. When he said that he didn't want to, she laughed and said they'd already done it, so what was he worried about? Thinking she had a point, Brad went along with it, but now he's avoiding her texts.

2. Jo has recently started dating Leah, who identifies as a lesbian but hasn't told anyone yet. Jo has been out and proud for five years now. She is really into Leah and as a tactile person, she expresses her feelings through affectionate gestures like rubbing her shoulders, linking her arm around her waist, and kissing her hair. Leah loves this in private but has told Jo not to be affectionate in public because she isn't out yet. But Jo can't help herself, and when the girls are at the mall, she keeps reaching out for hugs, cheekily pinches Leah's backside, and ruffles her hair.

Brad and Yasmin didn't have any boundaries, or indeed a relationship, when they first met, but that doesn't mean they can't set them afterward. Leah clearly expressed her boundaries to Jo, who dismissed her without giving a second thought to who might see them and what consequences that might have for Leah. Both Brad and Leah are dating people who don't respect their choices, and they need to either speak up more clearly for what they want or move on to people who will listen. It doesn't matter what form unwanted physical contact takes; if you violate someone's personal space, it's a serious breach of their trust.

## Emotional

1. Chloe has been in a relationship with Woody for the past year. Woody is having a difficult time at home and will often call Chloe at all hours to vent about his dad. He says he doesn't know how he'd get through the day without her there because she is his rock and he loves her. Chloe just got accepted to her first-choice college in another state, but she's wondering if she should turn it down because she's worried about how Woody will react when he finds out she's planning to leave.

2. Lennon and Tilly have been sending flirty messages over the weekend, but when they saw each other at school on Monday, Tilly was surprised that Lennon didn't mention it. However, he texted her again that evening and the flirting continued. Tilly's heart races every time her phone beeps and she finds herself checking it all the time in case she's missed anything. Lennon

asked her out on a date for Friday, but then Tilly overheard another girl in her class talking about a date she went on with Lennon on Wednesday night and now she feels crushed.

Romantic relationships form quickly and you can find yourself falling head over heels straight away, which is what has happened to Ava. The relationship is so new that they haven't had a chance to talk about their expectations yet, and it sounds like Lewis doesn't want commitment, whereas Ava is already acting like he's her boyfriend. Lack of communication about their boundaries and what is acceptable has led to Ava getting hurt.

Looking at the first example, it seems like the relationship is very one-sided. Woody expects Chloe to support him emotionally and is putting pressure on her to prioritize his needs—even if he doesn't realize it. This is a classic example of a co-dependent relationship, where one partner relies on the other without reciprocating.

## What Are Your Limits?

Building expectations into your relationships is the best way to keep them healthy and happy, but it's a step that people often leave out, especially if they lack confidence or experience. If it's your first relationship, you might be unsure about the right time to talk about this. It takes a certain level of comfort and intimacy to want to start discussing feelings and boundaries, so it might not be a good idea to open your first date with "I would like it if we texted every day."

Some boundaries you will discover through experience, but others you will already have a pretty good idea of. You might know that you don't want to have sex outside of marriage, so your boundaries around physical contact will be set from the outset. The thought of public displays of affection might make you cringe, or you might be expecting hugs, kisses, and holding hands to be an everyday part of your relationship. Whatever your expectations, as shown by some of the examples above, if your relationship doesn't meet them, it can feel pretty upsetting.

## Negotiable Boundaries

While some of your boundaries will be set in stone, you will find that others are more fluid. Maybe you initially want to keep the relationship private, but after a few weeks, you both feel comfortable telling close friends. It's really important to talk about any changes to make sure that your partner is happy too. If they aren't, you'll have to stick to the original expectations or find a happy medium.

Big changes in your life can also force you to adjust your boundaries. If one of you moves away, for example, you'll both need to rethink how often you communicate and whether you want to open the relationship up to dating others while apart and being committed when you are back together. If you've been dating casually and want to move to an exclusive, committed relationship, that's going to change your expectations, so it's really important to talk with your partner about what you think your new relationship will look like.

## How to Communicate Your Needs

The only way to effectively set boundaries in your relationships is to talk about them with your partner. You might not know each other very well, especially at the start of a relationship, so trying to guess what they want is impossible. And because people at the beginning of a relationship often try to keep the other person happy, they may not always tell the truth about what they like. As a teenager, I once gave a girlfriend a stuffed penguin because she wore a t-shirt with one on our first date. "That's so cute, I love it," was her response, and so from then on, every gift I bought her had a penguin theme. When she broke up with me, I found out the t-shirt belonged to her sister and she was never that into penguins; she was being polite. Penguin gifts aren't normally a boundary you need to set; the point is that if you politely let someone do something, they might then assume that it's okay. For instance, that could mean you are inundated with penguins, and therefore, they keep holding your hand or expecting you to answer immediately when they text.

## Lead with I

It's very easy to feel that someone setting a boundary is a sign that you've done something wrong. But even if you did, you didn't know because that boundary hadn't been set yet, so you can have a free pass on the guilt. To help reduce that emotional reaction, start setting your boundaries with statements beginning with "I."

- "Don't hold my hand when we're at school." This makes it sound like your partner has done something wrong.

- "I don't feel comfortable with public displays of affection, so I'd rather we didn't hold hands at school." This clearly explains how you feel and shows that this boundary comes from your feelings and not something your partner has done.

- "You can't tell anyone that we're dating." This makes your partner wonder why you're ashamed of them.

- "I'm not ready to go public yet. If my parents found out, they wouldn't be happy because I'm supposed to be focusing on my exams." This gives good reasons for setting this boundary; although,

I guarantee your parents will work out that something is going on. You're not as good at hiding stuff as you think you are.

Another reason for expressing boundaries by telling your partner what you feel is because it's difficult for them to argue with you! If you tell them that they're texting you too much, they can disagree and turn it around, saying you aren't texting enough. But if you say you feel that they're expecting too much communication, they should accept your feelings. If they still demand to be able to get hold of you any second of the day, even if it's making you uncomfortable, then maybe you two aren't compatible.

## It's Not All About You

Your partner probably has some boundaries that they want to set too. Hopefully, they'll feel comfortable coming out and telling you, but if they don't, you should definitely ask them. And if they ask you first, what a wonderful sign that they're interested in your feelings and making sure you're comfortable—you hit the jackpot!

Part of your growing intimacy as a couple is that you should be able to talk to each other about what makes you comfortable and the things that you need from each other. After you've explained your boundaries and expectations, turn it into a dialogue by asking for theirs. Not sure how? Try these conversation starters:

- I want to respect your boundaries. Would you like to tell me what they are?

- Are you okay with how much we talk/see/touch each other, or would you like more/less?

- Is there anything that's nonnegotiable for you while we're dating?

- Is it okay if I do this?

## What if You Don't Agree?

It's perfectly natural that there will be times when you both want different things. One of you may want to spend every spare moment together, but the other one wants to divide their time between their partner and their friends. By discussing these expectations, you have a chance to reach a compromise; if you don't see each other on the weekend, you can agree to video chat instead. If you don't talk about things, you'll both end up frustrated when your expectations don't match.

If you can't reach a compromise—or if your partner insists on sticking with their opinions and ignoring yours—it's probably a huge flashing neon sign that you should go your separate ways. No matter how strong the attraction between you is, this romantic relationship has no future if your values and needs are so different.

# Chapter Four

---

# **Get Consent, Give Respect**

*S*ILENCE DOES NOT MEAN *yes.* –Amy Reed

Teenage relationships are full of firsts and new experiences on both sides. This is a new type of relationship that you haven't had before, although you will have seen plenty of examples from people in your life, books, TV, movies, and the media. There are loads of new milestones to hit, including first dates, first kisses, and the first time meeting parents. When you first start dating, these might be new to you both at the same time, but the older you get, the more likely it is that either you or your partner has got more experience than the other.

While it can be exciting discovering your relationship together, it's likely that you might want to move at different speeds in terms of how quickly your intimacy or commitment develops. It's so important to keep communicating and make sure that everyone gives their consent for activities, especially if one of you is more experienced than the other. And we're not just talking about sex here, although you definitely need consent for that.

We ask people's consent every day, in many small social interactions. Can I sit here? Does anyone mind if I take the last cupcake? Do you want to share a milkshake? Why would you behave differently in a romantic relationship when you're supposed to care about your partner and their feelings? Yet the intensity of your own feelings can make it easy to want to overrule what others want. Think about the following scenario:

*You've had a crush on a classmate for months and you were delighted when you were assigned to be science partners. You swapped numbers so you could chat about your joint project but ended up also talking about other things. You decide to ask them out and are delighted when they say yes—this is literally your dream come true and you are so happy, you could run up and down the street, shouting. But the next text that comes through asks you to keep it a secret. Okay, you promise, but the next day at school your best friend notices your goofy grin and starts prodding you for information. Then your brother makes a joke about a crush and you blush, so he asks you their name.*

Would you tell them? It's only a couple of people and you trust them to keep a secret; after all, they're your best friend and your brother. They just want to share in your happiness, and besides, you're so head over heels in love that you don't think you can hide it any longer or you'll burst.

See how your judgment can be clouded by your own feelings? Not only do you not have consent to reveal you're going on a date, but consent has actually explicitly been withdrawn. You don't know what consequences that not respecting that request could have. What if it had been the other way around? I imagine you would be furious. As irritating as it might be to have to keep the secret, it will strengthen the relationship and show that you can be trusted.

## Permission to Explore

You must have seen or heard some recent news stories that involve consent. Unfortunately, there are people out there who don't think that they need to obtain it, and cases involving rape and sexual assault are still far too frequently being reported. You may even have read or seen some posts online from men—you'll notice I try my hardest in this book not to specify genders within my examples, but this issue definitely comes from the male gender—who claim that it is becoming impossible to talk to or be friends with women, for fear of being accused of going against their consent. I'll deal with this topic in more detail in chapter five, but I'll give you a few very simple starting points:

- If you're going to do something that involves another person, they need to be okay with it.

- Always assume you do not have consent unless explicitly told otherwise.

What's the difference between bullying and joking with friends? The consent of the person at the butt of the joke. Calling your mate fat because he polished off a whole bucket of KFC is different from calling a random classmate fat for bringing nothing but donuts for lunch. Ribbing each other is probably an established part of your friendship—meaning overtime, you've all given your consent—but you don't have those relaxed boundaries with a stranger. Do you know if they'll be okay with it? No, so, assume you don't have their consent to make that joke.

## Ways to Communicate Consent

Now look, I get it; nobody walks around all day long asking people for their consent before they interact with them. As you get older, you get better at navigating situations where consent is implied, and for the majority of social situations, that's perfectly fine, because we can all be rational grown-ups. I may not want to chat with the cheerful stranger while we're waiting for the bus, and they won't have asked my consent before saying hi, but at the end of the day, they're just being friendly and it doesn't cause any harm to chat back. If I really want to avoid others, I'll put my earbuds in or bury my nose in a book.

Why, then, does everyone seem to be stressing to teenagers that getting consent is so important if adults don't always follow their own advice? Again, it comes down to experience. Remember: Dating is still a whole new experience for you, and having the confidence to turn around in the heat of the moment and say, "No, I don't want to do this," is really hard. By emphasizing how important it is to gain consent, it takes the pressure off the person who may not want to give it.

Lots of people find asking for something they want—whatever the situation—daunting. Imagine you're sitting by yourself at a table in the school cafeteria and a group of friends sit down with you. They open a big bag of your favorite candy and start sharing it around. Now, to get a piece of their candy, one of two things has to happen:

1. They ask you if you would like a piece.

2. You ask them if you can have one.

If they don't ask you, how confident would you feel speaking up and asking for a piece yourself? What's the worse that can happen if you do? Probably that they say no and go back to ignoring you, and you don't get a piece of candy—so you're no worse off than before. But I still know a number of you would rather stay quiet. If you can't ask for a piece of candy, are you going to be able to ask your partner to stop doing something you don't like?

## How to Say Yes or No

When you're in the exciting stage of a new relationship, you'll probably want to spend lots of time with your partner. Add in some raging teenage hormones and that often leads to making out, cuddling, and sexual contact. It can be really helpful to take a minute—not in that situation, but when you're both thinking with your brains rather than any other organs—to talk about those physical boundaries and what you consent to. I don't mean you need to set out a six-month plan for how you see things progressing, but stick to those "I" statements to express your limits.

- "I feel really comfortable kissing you, but I want you to keep your hands above my waist."

- "I don't think I'm ready for you to see me naked yet, but if I get there, I will let you know."

- "We've been dating for a while and we're both 16 now, so I wanted to let you know that I'd like us to have sex, but only when you're ready. I might keep asking, but it's okay to say no. I'm not trying to pressure you; I'm just checking in."

If something starts happening that you are not happy with, you need to say stop. Not saying no is often read as saying yes, and it's definitely not the same thing. Don't worry about making your partner unhappy or uncomfortable, and don't worry about causing an argument. You need to put yourself first.

Another really important point to make is that you are free to withdraw your consent at any time. Just because you consented to the idea of something, doesn't mean you are going to like the reality, especially if it's not something you've ever tried before. I once ordered a spicy chicken dish at a restaurant because I liked the sound of it, but when it arrived, it was far too hot for me. Did I have to eat it just because I chose it? No, I realized it wasn't for me and I ordered a steak instead.

## Explicit Consent Versus Implied Consent

I've mentioned both explicit and implied consent already, but in case you're not sure exactly what each means, here's a quick rundown:

Explicit consent is usually verbal or written, and it is the use of specific words or actions to declare that you give your permission for something to happen. When you tick the box to agree to a mailing list's terms and conditions, for example, that's you giving your consent for them to contact you. Saying something like, "It's okay if you want to kiss me," is you giving your consent for someone else to, well, kiss you! There's almost no way to make a mistake with explicit consent; it's pretty obvious.

Implied consent often isn't verbal, and it's a way of giving consent for something to happen without coming out and saying it. It can sometimes be difficult to work out implied consent, especially in informal circumstances. If you turn up at A&E with an injury and ask for help, it's implied that you are giving the doctor consent to examine you, touch your injury, give you medication, and run tests. In relationships, we often read implied consent so that if someone acts one way to us, we can do the same. For example, if you reach out and hold someone's hand, they might reasonably assume that they can do the same to you in the future.

However, implied consent is frequently quoted in a number of situations where people think they have received it but have instead misread the signs. This is why it is important to always get explicit consent from your partner, especially as you add more physical intimacy to your relationship.

## Quiz Time!

Do you think you can tell whether consent was given in each of these situations?

1. Amy and Lewis, two 16-year-olds, met on social media through mutual friends. They have been texting, sexting, and video calling for a few weeks and both have told other people that they are dating. They eventually meet in person at a friend's birthday party. They've both been sexting about what they would do to each other if they met in person, and after a few alcoholic drinks, Lewis suggests they find a bedroom upstairs and follow through on their plans. Amy giggles and says they weren't real plans, but lets Lewis take her hand and lead her upstairs, where they finally get to have sex.

2. Taylor has recently got into the goth scene and they have started to wear a lot of corsets, fishnet jumpers, and heels. They feel super body confident for the first time in their life and are really happy with how they look. While out at the

bowling alley with a group of friends, some boys from another school start whistling at Taylor and blowing kisses. Taylor has never been whistled at by boys before and it makes them feel pretty and attractive. On the way back from the bathroom, they pass one of the boys, who makes a sexual gesture and grabs Taylor's ass as they walk past.

3. Jake (17) is recently out and hasn't had a lot of experience with gay relationships, although he has made several LGBT+ friends online. One of them, Ollie, asks Jake if he'd like to go on a date with his friend Malachi (19), and sends Jake a picture. Jake is nervous but says yes because Malachi is just his type, and Ollie insists they'll definitely get along. They have a great evening and Malachi even offers to drive Jake home. They kiss and then Malachi starts to unbutton Jake's jeans. "Ollie was right," he says with a smile, "you definitely know how to have fun. Let's keep it going." Jake doesn't want to spoil the fun so he lets Malachi perform oral sex on him.

4. Hattie is Marc's first girlfriend and although they don't go to the same middle school, they see each other every weekend. They message each other a lot, as well as video call almost every night. One night, Hattie and her friends are getting ready for the school disco, trying on different outfits and

doing their makeup. She takes a bunch of selfies pulling different faces, and her friends use her phone to take photos of her posing in her new dress. She sends all of these to Marc. Because he thinks she looks hot, he sends them on to some of his friends.

5. 18-year-old Maria's parents have gone away for the weekend and she invites over her boyfriend Diego. This isn't uncommon because they often visit her aging abuela in the next state over, and Diego is always happy to keep her company. They watch a romantic movie and order pizza before making out on the couch. Before too long, they are just wearing their underwear and involved in heavy foreplay. Maria asks Diego to stop. "Do you have a condom?" she asks him, and he pulls one out of his wallet.

6. Larissa has recently developed feelings for her friend Faye. They've known each other for years and hang out all the time. At a sleepover, they're playing "I Have Never" with a group of girl friends and Faye says "I have never kissed a girl." To Larissa's surprise, everyone else takes a drink (of Kool-Aid) and they all start teasing Faye that she should kiss one of them so she's not left out. Faye says okay and chooses Larissa. Later on, everyone else is asleep and Faye and Larissa are

lying next to each other, whispering about people they like at school. "You," says Larissa, and she pulls Faye in for a longer kiss.

None of the people in these examples asked for explicit consent, which they should have done—except for the boy in the second example; you shouldn't be grabbing strangers at all. But Lewis, Malachi, Diego, Marc, and Larissa all had the opportunity to check in with their partner, and it would only have taken a couple of seconds. It's worth it to be 100% sure that you're both into whatever comes next.

Think you spotted some implied consent in there? Only Maria and Diego gave implied consent; Maria by asking Diego to wear a condom, and Diego by having one. It shows that both of them had considered the idea of having sex and decided that, given the right circumstances, it was something they wanted to participate in.

Implied consent for physical contact is never given by:

- the type of clothing that someone wears
- whether they are drinking alcohol or taking illegal substances
- flirtatious behavior or texts, including pictures
- a previous relationship or previous physical contact

- their friends or other people

- the fact that they are talking to you or having fun with you

## When You Don't Feel Heard

Nobody should ever be made to feel uncomfortable and unheard by someone who is supposed to love or care deeply for them. Unfortunately, this isn't always the reality. If you are in a relationship with someone who doesn't ask for your consent or ignores you when you withdraw it, then they don't really care about you at all. The reason why I started this book by looking at self-respect and self-confidence is because these are the weapons that will help you to stand up for your values and your needs.

If you find yourself being ignored, start by having a specific conversation about the issue. Choose a time and place where you are both calm and rational. Don't replace another activity, because then your partner will turn up expecting something else that was planned and immediately feel resentful that they've been misled. Just agree to meet somewhere for a chat.

Crack out those "I" statements again to let them know that you feel that they aren't listening to your needs. You should probably expect some defensive arguments—people hate when they're told they've done something wrong, whether it was intentional or not—but stick to your guns. If things don't change, or if they do at the start but then quickly slip back into old ways again, then I'm afraid the relationship isn't working. No matter how much you are attracted to this person, if they won't give you the respect you deserve, they're not worth yours.

# Chapter Five

## **Meeting the Right People**

*You meet thousands of people and none of them really touch you. And then you meet one person and your life is changed... forever.* –Jake Gyllenhaal

Your social circle reaches much wider than mine ever did, and lots of today's teens are taking full advantage of their chances to meet as many people as possible. I suppose, the more people you meet, the higher chance you have of finding someone who takes your breath away. One of the best ways to do this is to get yourself out there.

- Join a sports team or an academic team, or just find a club that lets you develop a new hobby or passion. How about a choir, drama club, sewing circle, hiking club, or a Dungeons and Dragons group at the local library?

- Plan parties and outings with your friends and encourage them to invite some of their other friends. Accept invites to parties and gatherings, even if it seems a little scary at first. The more you go, the more you will start to recognize the other people there, and soon you won't feel like the odd one out anymore.

- Be open to conversation wherever you go. If you always hide at the back of the school bus, listening to music, you're missing out on the opportunity to talk to someone new on the ride home. The same goes for sitting in the lunch hall, in the park, or around the neighborhood.

- Find online groups based on your interests. You'll soon find something to chat about with the other people there. If you play online games, you might end up joining parties with the same people and becoming friends that way. There are also some online help groups for teens to talk to others who are going through the same things, like coming out, dealing with alcoholism in the family, or bereavement.

- Connect with friends of friends through social media. The algorithms are already programmed to suggest them to you; why not add some of the people to your own account? But it's worth checking with your friend whether the person you're talking with is someone they know in real life or whether they've only spoken to them online, the reason being that people who have never been seen outside of their socials might not be who you think they are.

## Never Compromise Your Safety

Thanks to the internet, you can connect with people from all over the world through shared interests and experiences. But with the ease of meeting people comes a number of new complications. We all want to assume the best scenario and give everyone the benefit of the doubt, but you need to retain some caution around online friends. Never give out any private information that could identify where you live, go to school, or hang out on a regular schedule. Try not to share photos from recognizable locations—you can always sort your friends into different lists, an inner circle and an outer one, to limit who sees what.

Romantic relationships can spark online too. Not only does everyone tend to post their best pictures, but they also have time to think of funny responses and good flirty comments. Not having someone sit in front of you often makes you feel more confident. You don't have to worry about hiding any blushes or if they're picking up on your subtle non-verbal cues.

Social media also makes it easier to lie about who you are. You can edit pictures, or post pictures of someone who you think is much more attractive than you and pretend they're yours. These aren't suggestions, by the way; I'm hoping to make you aware that there is always a possibility that the person you are talking to isn't actually that cute kid from the next school over. Best-case scenario: They're insecure about their looks and used a different photo. Worst-case scenario: They're an adult with some very bad intentions.

## Taking It Offline

If you've found someone online who you love talking to, it's natural to want to spend time with them offline too. If they're in a different continent, that's going to be very difficult, but lots of the people in your extended social circle are probably fairly local. But before you start making arrangements, you need to make sure you have put your safety first, just in case they aren't who they say they are. If you know that you have a safety net, you'll feel more relaxed and free to enjoy your date.

- Always meet in a public place, such as a coffee bar, park, or food court. Make sure there are plenty of people and the space is relatively open. Try and get a good view all around you and stay away from trees, pillars, or doorways. You don't want to give anyone an opportunity to sneak up on you or grab you from behind.

- Make sure people know where you are going and who you are meeting. Share your phone location and send a photo of you in your outfit to your friend, or post it to your social media. It might look like you're just checking that you look great, but it also means if anything happened to you, you're easy to identify and everyone knows exactly what you're wearing.

- Definitely tell your parents. You don't have to say it's a date if you don't want to, it could just be a friend meet-up, but make sure they know that you're meeting someone you haven't met before. Tell them if they're a friend of a friend, or if you met them online through social media or a forum. This is your chance to show them how mature you can be by explaining what precautions you've taken, or by asking them to hang around for a few minutes and wait just out of sight.

- Better still, go with a group of friends and their partners and have a mass date. There's definitely safety in numbers. Failing that, have a friend or two sit nearby so that they can keep an eye on you. You can even agree on using a secret signal if you want them to come over and "bump into you."

- If you're alone and no friends were available to come with you, you can always tell a barista, waiter, or shop worker that you're meeting someone from an app or online, and ask them to come over in 10 minutes to check if everything is okay. You can offer them a tip, but I'm sure any decent human being will be happy to watch out for you.

- Arrange for someone to call you, or for you to call them, at a set point in your date. Okay, it might look cheesy, but it's cool that someone has your back. If you want to be more private about it, nip to the bathroom for a quick check-in call, and drop a bit of gossip while you're there.

- Have your exit strategy planned, both for a successful and unsuccessful outcome. Make sure you have someone lined up to collect you, or if you have to take public transport, check out in advance where the bus stops are and what time the buses will be there. Make sure there's somewhere nearby you can wait, like a cafe, so that if your date follows you, it won't just be the two of you sitting at the bus stop.

- Don't be afraid to make a scene. Keep a clear route between you and the door in case you need to make a run for it. It's much better to escape loudly than to stay silently uncomfortable.

## Trust Your Gut

Once you and your date sit down and start talking, you might feel like you can tell the cavalry to stand down, but it's worth letting them hang on for a few more minutes. Just because the right person sits down across the table from you, doesn't mean their online persona is going to match their real personality. Your final safety catch should always be your gut feeling. If something seems off or doesn't feel right, even if you can't exactly put your finger on it, there's no need to stay. Even if this is your first date and you have nothing to compare it to, you are still capable of spotting red flags. Here are a few to get you started:

- They're rude to, or about, other people. Being short with café staff, complaining about other customers, or ranting about their exes are all signs that you should back away quickly. If they can't be nice to other people, it's highly likely they won't be very nice to you either.

- They only talk about what they've been up to and what they like. Everything you say gets turned around to be about them and their achievements. It sounds like they're not really interested in getting to know you, so you shouldn't care about getting to know them either.

- They repeatedly interrupt you, ignore you, or spend a lot of time on their phone. It's really disrespectful, and you deserve better.

- They don't respect your boundaries. Maybe they try to convince you to go somewhere else after you've said no or they want you to stay longer when you've said it's time to leave. If they're doing this on the first date, it's only going to go downhill from there.

- They try to move the date along too quickly. You might have been chatting for a while beforehand, but that doesn't mean you're ready to share a chair or have them draped all over you. Run especially fast if they already start talking about sex or planning important future events like prom, homecoming, or birthday parties. You've hardly spent five minutes together, these are not first-date topics!

- They mock any of your safety measures or try and get you to move to a different, unknown location. If they get upset about you wanting to feel safe, this is not a relationship you want to be in.

## It's Not All Doom and Gloom

I don't mean to make it sound like everyone you meet online is out to kidnap you, bully you, or pressure you into something you don't want to do, but it happens frequently enough that everyone needs to be aware of it. Probably the worst that will happen to you is your date turns up looking nothing like their (very old) photo, only talks about themselves, and insists you pay the whole bill.

However, if you've been comfortably chatting away online, exchanged numbers, or even had some video calls, then meeting this person in real life could be a magical experience. There's nothing like the rush of finally meeting your crush and getting to hold them, and it will send the butterflies in your stomach into overdrive. With all your safety checks in place, you're sure to have a truly wonderful time, especially if you talk about your boundaries and expectations beforehand.

## The Curse of Social Media

Social media is an incredibly new phenomenon that has become such an important part of many people's lives that it's hard to imagine life beforehand. How on earth did people keep track of what their old schoolmates were doing before Facebook, Instagram, and TikTok? Where did you share jokes, memes, and cat videos?

It's entirely possible that your caregivers went through their teenage years without social media, a mobile phone, or even reliable home internet. Social media, in one form or another, has always been around for you, whether you have actively used it or are just aware of its existence. It helps you communicate with your friends in ways that older generations never did and just don't understand. This can make it difficult for them to see the benefits, focusing instead on the downsides: too much screen time, an influx of uncontrolled content, and the fact that mistakes made online are never fully erased.

If social media has completely changed the way your generation views and interacts with the world, imagine what it has done to the public view of relationships. I know of several people who are having trouble in their relationships, but you'd never know that from the smiling pictures on their Instagram feeds. The internet lets you present whatever view of your world you want others to see, hiding the bad times and only showing your best side.

But that view of the world isn't healthy. When you're surrounded by images of people on their best days, with their best hair and their best outfits, you start to believe that that's what they're like all of the time. So, when your life hits a bump in the road, you feel like you're the only one that isn't happy, and that means there must be something wrong with you. I promise you, you're not alone, you're just experiencing your own life without a filter.

The moral of the story? Take everything you see on social media with a heavy pinch of salt. Not everyone is as happy or in love as they look, not everyone is coupled up, and those that are do not have amazing dates all the time. No one wants to share the failures, the down moments, or the bad hair days, so always treat social media like the highlights reel that it is.

## When the Internet Goes Dark

As wonderful as the internet is for bringing people to-gether and helping you to research your history assign-ment, in the wrong hands, it can be extremely dangerous. As much as we can try to police it and make sure that only helpful and positive content is posted, the internet is just far too large to find everything. Then there's the huge issue of people's right to have freedom of speech, something that is really important, but also needs to be treated responsibly. Your school might already have told you to be careful about what information you use for your essays, but what about your own personal re-search?

## Opinion or Misinformation?

The worst thing about the internet is that people can post whatever they want without anyone checking it. Can you imagine if that happened at school? You could make up all of your assignments and talk about chemicals that didn't exist or events that never happened. And if you told all your friends, they could do it too. Except some of them might add even more details, and soon you've all created a fictional country and its little-known cheese-based civil war of 1850 that led to its downfall. Next year, a new bunch of kids have to write the same assignment, and they've seen your work displayed on the walls or heard it read out as a good example, so they write about it too, adding some embellishments of their own. By the time your own kids go to that high school, they're teaching an entire module about your country, its people and customs, and how its self-destruction is a lesson to us all.

Sounds ridiculous, doesn't it? But stuff like that happens on the internet every day. Even major news networks have fallen into the trap of reporting someone's opinion—or even someone's social media joke—as real news. If they can't tell the difference, how are you supposed to?

If you've got a question that you think is personal, embarrassing, or just too weird to ask your friends or caregivers, who do you turn to? It's probably Google, but which of the hundreds of results is going to give you the right answer? Or, if you post it anonymously to Reddit,

Quora, or another forum, how can you be sure that the advice you're getting is helpful? One way is to look at the type of website you're reading from. For medical advice, it's always best to look for sites provided by your country's health service, hospitals, or registered charities. They should give you accurate information and links to further people who can help. And for the really personal stuff? You're best off making an appointment with a local health professional to talk in person. That way you can be sure that you're getting the right advice for your situation.

## Online Grooming

Being able to hide your identity online can be a good thing. If you're investigating your sexuality, wanting to talk about experiences with abusive partners, or looking for answers to personal questions, taking shelter behind an anonymous username can give you strength and courage. But there are other people online who use their anonymity to lie about their age, gender, location, and intentions. Some people will try and tell you that their actions are harmless—like using someone else's photos to catfish people on dating apps because you don't feel attractive as yourself—but this is never a victimless activity, and whether you intended to or not, someone will end up upset.

Other people have more sinister motives. Pedophiles can pretend to be children and teenagers in order to form close relationships that are forbidden and illegal. This is known as grooming, and the people who do it are very skilled manipulators. You might think you're sending cute selfies to someone in your year in the next town over, but you can never really be sure where your images are actually going to end up. Always be skeptical when talking to strangers online and never give out personal details or send photos. Set your social media accounts to private and only accept friend requests from people you know or have invited.

Another type of online grooming that is worryingly growing in prevalence is from groups who spread misinformation, prey on the emotional vulnerability of teens, and promise radical solutions to others' problems. You might have heard the term incel, or some of the vocabulary they use to talk about people, such as alpha and beta males. This group of men—yes, this is the group I mentioned in chapter four—are unhappy, and they blame this unhappiness on women. They can't get a date and women won't talk to them, so they express this as hatred toward any man who can get a date and all women. It sounds petty, but to your teenage boys who don't fit the type of typically attractive or interesting to girls, it can feel like they have found a group who understand them. Incels encourage boys to talk disparagingly about women and girls, showing a lack of respect and trying to make girls feel bad for how they look and act, or how many boyfriends they've had.

All kinds of grooming starts small; sharing memes and jokes, doling out quips and pithy statements, and flattering their targets. But then things start to get more intense. If you're worried that you or your friends might be the subject of online grooming, either from a person pretending to be a teenager or from a group like the incels, then the best thing to do is to talk to a trusted adult about it. Cut all online contact and switch off the internet for a while. If it's a friend you are worried about—maybe they've started to spend more time online, but they hide what they're doing, or they mention a new person in their life but nobody else knows them or where they came from—don't try and investigate yourself. Make the adults aware and they will be able to talk to them and find out what, if anything, is going on.

## Internet Pornography

It's great how much stuff we can get for free online, right? YouTube is full of awesome comedy clips, videos teaching us how to do pretty much anything, and even complete episodes of TV shows from the good old days before Netflix. You can get news articles for free, research your school projects for free, access free software to video call friends and relatives halfway around the world, and even store your photos on the cloud for free. But the thing about all this free stuff is it's often unregulated. Those YouTube videos don't come with ratings like the movies, and there's no one to check that the facts you're reading are correct, or that halfway down the article, it doesn't suddenly change into a rant against the current government. And unless someone's turned on the safe search filter, there's nothing to stop anyone from searching for graphic images and movies.

The thing about pornography is that, like dating and sex, it offers something new and unknown, which teenagers feel is a window into a world that they have now unlocked. However, just like Hollywood sells you an idealized view of relationships, pornography is about as close to real sex as *Spongebob Squarepants* is to an undersea nature documentary. So, while being open about sex and normalizing age-appropriate sexual behavior is all positive and helps to remove feelings of guilt and shame, it's debatable whether porn has a role in this discussion.

Here are the main problems:

- Pornography is not the best way to learn about the ins and outs of sex, although it might seem like the perfect option; after all, we watch video tutorials to learn how to cook, how to get through a tough video game level, and how to learn

French vocabulary. But the reality is that it's wildly exaggerated, and it would be like trying to learn to drive by watching *The Fast and the Furious*!

• The majority of pornography depicts unrealistic behaviors and scenarios that are designed specifically to excite the viewer, but without knowing that, teens can come to view these as normal. If you watch a load of horror movies about teens getting murdered in the woods, you're naturally going to be conditioned to be a little wary of the woods because an expectation has been established. So, if you watch a bunch of porn clips where one partner dominates the other, this is going to be your reference point when you and your partner end up in bed together.

• Historically, porn tends to show us an unequal relationship, with one partner exacting more control over the other. While shifting control around can be fun for some people within a controlled fantasy, in a relationship, it is unhealthy. A donut every once in a while is a nice treat, but eat nothing but donuts every day and you're going to feel ill very quickly.

• Porn actors are specifically chosen for their bodies rather than their acting skills. This can quickly give you a warped view of what your body is expected to look like. As a teenager, you aren't going to have the same features as a mature adult, you're still growing and your body is shaping well into your 20s. But your teenage years are a delicate time for your self-image, and watching yet another thing that makes you feel down about yourself isn't going to help.

- These movies are designated as adult content, but online they can be found by anyone, and if your house doesn't have filters for age-restricted content on your internet, then you might even do so accidentally. Imagine being a child and learning that sex is even a thing by watching really explicit, up-close videos. Viewing porn at a young age can be damaging to your self-image and your views of others, and it can permanently skew your expectations of adult relationships.

It's a good thing that the majority of teenagers today are actually pretty savvy when it comes to the internet and its illicit wares. According to research, as many as 52% of you realize that porn doesn't accurately represent a loving sexual relationship, but that doesn't mean that you are still able to watch it with a complete sense of detachment. (Rothman, 2023). All in all, it's best to leave internet pornography alone. When you are an adult, if you want to make the choice to watch porn either alone or with your partner, there has been a push in recent years to produce content that is milder, aimed at couples, or more female-centric that can make you feel excited without peddling unhealthy attitudes.

\*\*\*

*"Thanks for coming this far. If you're enjoying this book, please consider leaving an honest review on your Amazon store.*
*Thank you,*
*Kev"*

**Teens' Guide to Dating**

## Teens' Guide to Dating

UK
Review

Click here

Thank you for your
review 🙏

# Chapter Six

---

# Are You Listening?

C OMMUNICATION TO A RELATIONSHIP *is like oxygen is to life.
Without it, it dies.* –Tony A. Gaskins Jr

There's absolutely no way you can have a healthy, functioning relationship without being able to communicate properly with each other, and that goes for romantic relationships, friendships, family relationships, and even your relationship with your teachers. That means you have to be able to listen to the other person as well as talk to them. You can't just go around telling everyone what to do and what you want; that's talking at people, not to them. They're not going to listen to you either, because they know you won't be listening to them. Like everything else in life, good communication is a bit of giving and taking.

## Why Communication Is Important in Relationships

When two people are in a relationship—any kind of relationship—they should stop thinking about their individual needs and do things that benefit both people. A lot of the time, these will be things you enjoy anyway: You and your friends hold regular game nights, or you and your partner have a TV show you love to discuss. Spending time on activities that you both enjoy is what brings you closer together and increases your bond. How do you find these joint activities? Communication!

Asking each other what you enjoy, listening to the answers, and working together to find compromises, builds intimacy as well as gives you loads of fun things to do. Do you both love movies? Have a date at the cinema! You love horror but they hate it? Compromise and find a second or third choice that you will both find interesting, like sci-fi or a romantic comedy. Insisting that you go with your choice is going to show that you aren't interested in their preferences, but being willing to try something that might not be your thing will show your partner that you really care about making them happy. I know, it can sometimes be a pain in the ass, but this is you being the super nice person you are, right?

## Getting Communication Right

Communicating with your partner doesn't just mean you tell each other your favorite food and always like their social media posts. It means being able to discuss your feelings and your needs within the relationship. I've already talked about "I" statements in previous chapters, and they are still the best way of getting your point across without making it sound like you're blaming your partner for something. Here are a few more top tips for how to let your partner know what you need:

- Speak up as soon as you can about things that bother you. If you've been letting them get your name wrong for a few weeks, it gets more awkward to try and correct them later than if you'd pointed it out immediately! The same for whether you want less cuddling, more video calls, or really hate that they keep taking you to see scary movies.

- Be really clear about what you're saying, including what you need from them. Don't say, "That thing, last time, um, I'd rather not." Instead say, "I felt uncomfortable when you put your hand on my knee at the movies. Instead, you can hold my hand or put it around my shoulders." An "I" statement, a clear description of what you didn't like, and a suggestion about what to do instead—perfect!

- Don't yell, cry, or get over-emotional, and your partner is less likely to react that way in response. If they don't listen to you, or if they tell you that your feelings are silly and refuse to cooperate, then you are free to shout and stomp all you want!

- Relationships need to be built on trust, so if your partner tells you that they feel a certain way, you need to trust that they are telling the truth, rather than assuming there's an ulterior motive. In return, they should do the same for you.

- Let them ask you non-judgemental questions, like "What can I do instead?" or "Can I hold your hand if we're not in public?" It might be that you think you've been clear, but actually, there is more information that they need in order to understand where you're coming from. As long as their questions stay respectful and don't push you for details you aren't comfortable revealing, there's no reason why you shouldn't answer them.

## It's Not Just About Talking

When you have something really important to say, it often seems scarier to have the conversation in person rather than over texts, email, or even on the phone. But it's worth doing because the chances of a misunderstanding are much lower. What is said is as important as how it is said; the tone of voice and body language can often tell you so much more than words. Also, there's no point in talking if no one is listening. Having the other person physically with you can make it easier for them to hear what you're saying and properly take it all in.

## How to Listen

Now, you might be thinking that this is the most pointless section ever. After all, you've been listening to everything since you were born—unless you are hard of hearing, in which case you've been listening as long as people have been signing to you. The point is, there's a subtle difference between hearing and listening. You might hear your teacher telling you about the homework, but did you listen? Hearing is passive; it happens anyway if you have functioning ears, but listening is a more active sense. Listening means you pay attention; you take information in, digest it, understand it, and react to or act upon it. Some people will hear the teacher but almost instantly forget about the assignment. Those who listen will understand that they need to produce some work, they will remember the details and the deadline, and they will improve their relationship with the teacher by following their instructions. I always thought I listened properly, but when I became a cop, I realized I hadn't been listening as carefully as I thought. Suddenly, I had to learn to listen all over again so I could read situations before they got out of hand.

If you're in a relaxed conversation with your friends or your partner, and you're listening to them, you are more likely to keep information about the conversation. This will help you to remember things that they said they liked, what they want to do, or what they are looking forward to. A great way to surprise someone you care about is by remembering something little that they said and acting upon it another time. A friend of mine was on a third date with her boyfriend when he secretly slipped a new CD into the car's player. The previous week, she had casually mentioned that it had been on her Christmas list but no one had bought it for her. He instantly racked up some major boyfriend points, and all he'd really done was listen to something she said.

Knowing how to listen properly is useful in casual conversation, but it's absolutely vital for those talks where you're setting boundaries or discussing expectations and the future of your relationship. You're going to be giving each other a lot of new and important information. You're going to need to listen to every statement and process it before giving your reply.

Here's an example of a typical casual conversation:

Tim: "I saw the new Marvel movie last night. It wasn't as good as *Avengers Endgame*, but it was still pretty exciting."

Marc: "Yeah? I'm hoping to go see it next weekend, so don't tell me any spoilers!"

Tim: "I have to spend next weekend revising for my geography test."

Marc: "Bummer. I'm glad I took history instead. Maps make my head spin."

Notice how each reply isn't building on the one before? The chat just switches between the two people and their own experiences and activities: Tim did something, Marc wants to do it, Tim has to work, and Marc is glad he doesn't. They're hearing enough to notice a detail or two about what was said and relate it to something they've done. There's nothing wrong with this, it's how most conversations play out in everyday life, and as they aren't saying anything that really needs to be remembered, this is fine.

Here's a deeper conversation. This time our two characters are discussing their relationship, see if you can tell how it flows differently because they are both listening properly.

Tim: "I get really frustrated when you leave my messages on read. I can't help but think that you're ignoring me."

Marc: "I didn't realize you thought that. I read them whenever I can, but I like to make sure I give you a proper reply, so sometimes that has to wait."

Tim: "I don't mind if you just like it or send an emoji. Then you can reply later, and my stupid brain won't be overthinking things."

Marc: "Good idea, I hadn't thought of that. I'll try and remember for next time."

You can see that they're really listening to each other because each reply only makes sense after the comment before it. The conversation has an opening point and a final conclusion because the entire thread is a progression. That's only possible when people listen, rather than just hear.

## What About Body Language?

Body language means all the nonverbal signals that you use when you're talking with others. It can include different facial expressions, gestures, posture, and whether you hold eye contact or look at your feet. Reading someone's body language can tell you a lot about what they're thinking, feeling, and whether their intentions are honest. Understanding these nonverbal cues can give you additional context and help you better understand what someone is trying to say. For example, if you ask your partner what they were doing last night and they reply while fidgeting and avoiding eye contact, it might mean that they're not telling you the truth. If you're talking to your crush, and they lean into the conversation, find an excuse to touch your arm, and laugh at your jokes (even if they're really not that funny), it sounds like you should probably go ahead and ask them out.

Getting to know the nonverbal signs of someone being uncomfortable is really important. It will make sure you don't accidentally put your partner in a situation where they don't feel safe, disrespected, or ignored.

- Folded arms across the chest can mean that someone is uncomfortable and trying to create a barrier between themselves and you.

- If the person that you're talking to or sitting with is leaning away, it shows that they're uncomfortable with you being that close or with the topic of conversation.

- Avoiding eye contact or looking around the room could mean that they're trying to find a way out of the conversation.

- Some people fidget out of habit, but nail-biting, shifting weight from one foot to the other, fiddling with their hair, or twisting their fingers together could also be signs that your partner is feeling nervous or uncomfortable.

- Tensed muscles, like the jaw, fingers, or arms are another sign of discomfort.

All body language should be taken in context. For example, folded arms could also mean that they're cold, and a clenched jaw is a very common sign of anger, but as a general rule, if you spot some of these signs, you might want to take a step back, give them some space, and check in to see if they're okay. If you're talking about where your relationship is going, and your partner agrees to one thing, but their body language is giving you the feeling that they're uncomfortable, you should definitely pause and reconsider.

Here's an example: You've been dating your partner for a month now and you know that you have very strong feelings for them. You want them to come for dinner after school and meet your family. They say okay, but as you describe what is being planned for dinner, you notice them take a small step backward, shuffle their feet, and glance at the door.

Now, they might be worried about missing their bus, or they could be feeling nervous about this next step in the relationship. It's best to try and find out, so you could say something like, "I noticed you don't look very comfortable right now. Would you like to tell me what you're thinking?" Hopefully, they'll open up and be honest with you about their true feelings. If not, at least you gave them the opportunity.

## Saying What You Need

When you're with your friends, you probably feel completely comfortable speaking your mind. If you don't want to go to the park, or you've already seen the film they're talking about (and didn't really like it), there's no way you'll feel like being dragged along anyway. You'll be okay telling them that, and they'll either plan something else (yay, compromise!) or be fine with you doing your own thing instead. So, why is it so much harder to tell a romantic partner that you don't want to do something? This is someone who is supposed to care about you and your feelings and who wants to make you feel happy. They should be okay with whatever you say, too.

## Why There's So Much Drama

In reality, this isn't always the case. I've mentioned already that heightened emotions (and hormones) can exaggerate people's reactions, so any disappointment can be crushing. Say you were looking forward to a date with someone you really fancied, you had a lovely time, and at the end, you leaned in for a kiss. You'd been thinking about kissing them all evening, your heart is beating fast, and your stomach is doing somersaults, but instead of leaning in to meet you, they step back and tell you that they had a really nice time, but they're not ready for that yet. No matter how much you tell them that it's okay and you respect their decision, you're probably dying inside from a mixture of embarrassment and rejection.

You're not alone. It's a perfectly typical teenage reaction because your brain can't process anything rationally. If you could look inside an adult's brain, you'd see that most of their decisions are made in the prefrontal cortex, right at the front of the brain. It's the logical center and helps you to see the consequences and outcomes of your actions, as well as helps to control your impulses. This is why you see fewer adults throwing temper tantrums, and why they seem to always make boring, sensible decisions.

By contrast, your prefrontal cortex isn't really working yet. During your teenage years, it goes through some remodeling, ready for its adult role, and this involves forging lots of new nerves and neural connections. While it's under construction, your decisions are coming from your amygdala. It does its best, but the amygdala is like the anti-prefrontal cortex: It's ruled by emotions and impulses. This is why you find yourself getting really upset, angry, or happy over small things, and why it always seems like a good idea to do crazy stuff.

## Finding the Right Time

So, yeah, when someone turns around and tells you they don't want to do something, it can seem like a major rejection. Asking them beforehand makes this much less of a big deal because you're not being stopped in the moment. In fact, it's a good idea to set aside a time to talk about your feelings and expectations so you can manage the conversation. Trying to talk about things at the beginning of the date could end up meaning you don't have as much fun afterward. Bringing things up after something has happened, means your chat is going to be surrounded by lots of—possibly negative—emotions, and neither of you is going to be listening as closely as you need to.

It's a good idea to sit down together fairly close to the beginning of your relationship. Even if you're just planning on going on the occasional date, it's worth setting that expectation from the start. Be clear that you're meeting up to talk about boundaries and expectations so that there's no confusion about this being a date or some sort of fun activity. And do meet in person so that you have each other's full attention and there's no frustration about dropped Wi-Fi or bad signal.

Make sure each of you thinks about what you want to say beforehand, but also make sure you're prepared to hear everything that the other person says. They're most likely going to say things that aren't what you want to hear—it's not common for two different people to be on exactly the same page right at the start of their relationship—and if you're prepared for this, your emotional responses are going to be more manageable.

If you follow all these steps, you will set the stage for a really open and healthy discussion about your relationships, giving it the best start. With these in place, you know you can have fun and be comfortable in each other's company, without worrying about having your boundaries overstepped or not being listened to when it matters.

## What if They Don't Listen to Me?

Unfortunately, there are multiple reasons why your sensible requests might fall on deaf ears. Your partner might not have a lot of experience in relationships and making compromises, and they might find it too difficult to manage their emotions around this. They could still be a little immature, and feel that they want to be selfish about having a relationship that fits their vision, not someone else's.

At the end of the day, are you going to be happy with someone who doesn't listen to your thoughts and feelings? Are you going to be happy with a relationship that doesn't fit what you want? No matter how much you are attracted to them, and how much fun you have when you're together, if there are fundamental issues with communication, boundaries, and understanding, this relationship is never going to be anything more than a few fun dates. And if you try and stick it out, you're going to end up feeling miserable and frustrated. Imagine sitting down to watch your favorite movie, only to realize that you've got an edited version and half the scenes are missing. That's what it's like sticking in a relationship where you're not getting everything you want from it.

# Chapter Seven

## Endgame Goals: A Healthy Relationship

*Y*OU KNOW YOU'RE IN *love when you can't fall asleep because reality is finally better than your dreams.* –Dr. Seuss

If you're new to dating and you don't have any experience being in a relationship, how do you know if yours is working or not? Sometimes it's easy to tell, especially if being together is easy and the pair of you are always on the same page, but other times you might have a disagreement, or full-blown argument, or suddenly find yourself in a place where you're unable to see each other's point of view. Does this mean it's over?

Having disagreements in relationships is perfectly normal; it's all part of effective communication, and as you spend more time together, you're more likely to eventually annoy each other! I said back in chapter two that relationships involve a lot of intimacy and passion. After a while, the passion dies down and this is often when the cracks start to show. You both need to decide whether to introduce more commitment to your relationship to keep it going, or whether it has run its course.

## When Relationships Go Right...

My aim in this chapter is to paint you a detailed picture of a happy relationship so that you see what to aim for and so you recognize the signs of unhealthy behavior before it's too late. Although the finer details of every romantic relationship will be different—how often you see each other, whether you have date nights out or mostly stay in, the fact that you mostly communicate as characters from Lord of the Rings—there are a number of core characteristics under all these that should be absolutely nonnegotiable.

## Early Relationship: From Crushing to Dating

It's hard to describe the feeling of having a crush if you haven't felt it before, but there's nothing about it you can control. You might be walking around, minding your own business, and suddenly realize you've developed a thing for your best friend, the class clown, or even your teacher! A crush can come completely out of the blue, or it can build slowly overtime, but that doesn't mean you are aware of it happening. When you see your crush, your brain sends out waves of hormones called dopamine and oxytocin that make you feel happy and excited. Your brain loves the way these chemicals feel, so it tells you to see that person again so it can have another hit. That's right; your brain is a bit of an addict!

You'll find that seeing your crush, or even just thinking about them, will make you feel a bit giddy. Your heart rate can increase, your stomach feels like it's full of butterflies, and you might start sweating or blushing. You could also find that your legs feel a bit wobbly and you can't quite think of the right words to say. All of this, of course, makes you extremely attractive to them... not! Unfortunately, getting into a state over your crush isn't anything you can change, but hopefully, if you talk to them, they'll recognize all these signs that you really like them, and if they like you back, you can arrange a first date.

It's worth noting at this point that there are a lot of different things that can make you develop a crush on someone: feeling close to them, finding out something surprising about them, enjoying their company, thinking they are physically attractive, and going through similar experiences. Crushes are never really based on a solid foundation of experiences and communication with the other person; if they were, we'd never get them on celebrities, and they're often one of the most common targets. Crushes often involve a lot of fantasy—you start imagining what it would be like to talk to, spend time with, or kiss your crush—and this further fuels the crush itself. Remember that if you do manage to go on a real date with them, most of the time, it won't live up to your dreams.

At this point in your very new relationship, you're feeling a lot of passion for this person, but you don't really know each other yet, so the intimacy part is missing. This means you don't yet know much about their likes and dislikes or how they react in different situations. It can make you feel nervous before meeting up, even though you're also excited to see them. It's your brain playing tricks again; it wants the high of happy hormones that happens when you see your crush, but it's also making you feel a little worried, as they're still an unknown quantity. You don't know if they like candy or popcorn with their movie, or if they will share their haul or keep it to themselves. Will they be overly emotional and laugh, cry, or jump at all the right points, or will you be laughing by yourself? What if they're a noisy eater?

With so much not known about your crush (except the exact shade of their hair or how their eyes sparkle in the sunlight), it's best to go into the date with a completely open mind. Enjoy that you are learning new things about them and that you get to share some things about yourself too. Make sure you use your newly developed listening skills to remember what they are interested in and what they like, so you will know for next time. It's perfectly normal for the first few dates to feel a little awkward, as you're both getting a feel for each other and how you work as a couple—*if* you work as a couple.

This is also the best time to set some of those boundaries we talked about earlier. Talk together about the pace you'd like your relationship to move at, if there are any absolute no-go areas, and if there's anything that has happened so far that you haven't liked. The conversation might feel a little forced, especially if you're still building up your intimacy in the relationship, but surely an awkward ten minutes is worth it if it will ensure a healthier relationship, right?

If you're picking up this book as a young teenager (13-15), your early relationship will probably take place more over messaging apps and while at school because you're limited more by adults, as they will often call all the shots, like saying who is allowed to visit. Older teens (16+) might find that they have more autonomy about where they spend time with their partner, and it's even more important that they talk about their boundaries because their relationship might move more quickly toward physical intimacy.

## Established Relationship: Officially a Couple

After you and your partner have been dating for a while, your relationship will have built up a more solid foundation. This is created out of shared experiences, fond memories, aligned values, and a growing commitment toward each other. Your partner might not have the same brain-melting effect on you now that you know them a bit better, but while they no longer have you tongue-tied or going weak at the knees, you now enjoy their company for real rather than dreaming about a fantasy version.

At this stage, if your relationship is built on healthy values, there's no reason why it shouldn't thrive for as long as you both want it to. At the core of every successful relationship, teenage or adult, you should be able to spot the following traits:

- Trust. Both partners should trust the other to be reliable, predictable, and responsible. It's not just about not cheating on your partner (although that is extremely important); you need to be able to trust that you can talk to your partner and have them keep your secrets, follow your requests, and basically behave like your friend.

- Respect. This goes hand in hand with trust. You can't trust someone that doesn't respect you, because they won't care about your feelings or abide by your decisions. Respect means that you treat everything that is important to your partner as if it was just as important to you.

- Kindness. It should be obvious that being in a relationship with someone means you care about them, their well-being, and their happiness, and that means you should always be kind to each other. Even in the heat of an argument, you should avoid saying things that you know will leave a lasting scar, and you should never try and force your partner to do something that you know crosses a boundary.

- Support. Your partner's dream might not be the same as yours, but you should support them to do things that are important to them. In return, they should offer your support to achieve your goals or overcome your problems. It might be as simple as listening to them offload their troubles, or it might mean going to their recitals, games, or performances.

- Communication. This is the backbone of every relationship, whether romantic or platonic. It doesn't mean you need to talk to each other every day; it means that you feel comfortable talking about what matters and you know that your partner will listen to you without criticism.

- Commitment. Both of you need to agree that you will put time and effort into the relationship. If it's always the same person chasing the other to spend time together, it might mean that their heart really isn't in it. Making a commitment to another person doesn't mean you have to drop everything else you enjoy and only spend time with them, but it means you both need to agree to talk or spend time together on a regular basis; otherwise, things will fizzle out.

## ... And When They Don't

The perfect relationship probably won't happen for you straight away, unless you're very lucky. For some people, it never comes along. However, every relationship you have, although maybe not perfect, should at least be healthy and make you happy. Unfortunately, there are lots of people out there who end up in unhealthy relationships. These tend to occur when one or more of the key foundations mentioned above are missing.

Some unhealthy relationships don't start out like that, but overtime something shifts. Others are bad from the start. This can be the fault of one person or both partners, but whatever happens, it's important to recognize the red flags once they appear. This will give you the chance to either sit down together and try and work on what is missing, or let you walk away.

Common signs of an unhealthy relationship include:

- dishonesty and lying. It's one thing to tell you that top looks good on you when actually it doesn't; it's another thing to tell you that they're visiting grandma when they're really out partying with friends. Habitually lying to you about where they are, what they're doing, and how they feel, removes the trust from the relationship.

- wanting to control the other. This means they make all the decisions in the relationship, refuse to compromise, and may use emotional blackmail to force their partner to do something. Some examples would be: always having to go to their house and never having them come to yours, being made to feel guilty for spending time with your friends instead of them, or having them call you in an emotional state and dragging you away from your other plans.

  - Another kind of controlling behavior is extreme dependence. In an unhealthy relationship, one partner might convince the other that they can no longer live without them and threaten to hurt themselves if they don't get enough attention or if the relationship ends.

This makes the other partner feel guilty about spending time with friends or family and coerces them into always putting their partner first.

- constant monitoring of your whereabouts. If your partner insists you reply immediately or asks you to keep sending pictures of where you are and who you're with, this is a form of control. In extreme cases, they may even befriend you on social media using fake accounts, to see if you're hiding any posts from them.

- disrespect. Any behavior that involves making fun of your partner, teasing them about things that upset them, not listening to their boundaries, or constantly putting them down shows a complete lack of respect. This kind of behavior can start small and then escalate and is really insidious, often going unnoticed for some time. If you're the partner being disrespected, you can lose your self-esteem and your respect for yourself, believing overtime that you aren't worthy of anything and you deserve the abuse from your partner. This is never true, but as humans, we tend to believe negative things about ourselves much more than positive ones. If your friends start to tell you that you shouldn't put up with the way you're being treated, I urge you to listen to them.

○ It's really hard to respect someone who doesn't respect themselves, so if the relationship has degenerated to the point where the abusive partner has completely worn down the other, disrespect can grow into hostility and harassment. This can put the abused partner in physical danger if hurtful words become hurtful actions. There is never any reason why one partner should physically harm another, and if this happens to you, you need to tell a respected adult as soon as you can.

- feeling unsafe. At any point, if you don't feel safe in the company of your partner, this should be a clear sign that your relationship has serious problems. Feeling unsafe could include being worried about them physically hurting you, sexually assaulting you, emotionally threatening you, and intimidating you.

## Exit Strategies

If you've read through the information about unhealthy relationships and recognized some of the characteristics of your own, then I'm sorry you've not had a healthy, positive experience in your relationship. You might have known for a while that something wasn't right, or it might have just all fallen into place, but either way, you mustn't let it continue. You will be putting yourself in danger of emotional or physical trauma that can be difficult to recover from.

It isn't always as easy to break off a relationship as you might think, especially if your partner is exerting control or exhibiting threatening behavior. The most important thing to do is ensure your own safety. In some circumstances, that will mean leaving your partner immediately; in other cases, there might be things you should do first, especially if you think they will become violent toward you.

## Walking Away

The problem with unhealthy relationships is that the behavior of the controlling or abusive partner can make you feel worthless, at fault, and like you have failed them. It's hard to walk away from someone who scares you, but it's even harder to walk away from someone who manipulates you into feeling that no one better will ever want you. It's important for you to realize that neither they nor you can see into the future, and who knows where you will be in a couple of months or years. What is true is that no one deserves to be emotionally, physically, or sexually manipulated and abused, period.

If they threaten to hurt themselves as a result of you leaving, you should let a trusted adult know straight away.

## Protecting Yourself

"As you think about ending an unhealthy relationship, it's important to prioritize your safety, resources, and support system. If the person you're ending a relationship with has hurt you or threatened to hurt you in the past, plan for your safety and protect yourself from harm when preparing to end the relationship." (The Jed Foundation, n.d.). The Jed Foundation has some excellent advice for teens and young adults on how to end unhealthy relationships and their website is included among the references at the end of this book. Let's look at each of those important factors in turn:

- Think about your safety during and after the breakup. Don't do it in person if you're worried about your physical safety. Phone or text from a location where they wouldn't know to look for you. If you do it in person, make sure it is in a public location, and you have your phone, an exit strategy, and people who know where you are or are even there with you.

- After the breakup, change your routine as much as you can. Take a different bus, walk a different route to school, and change your shifts at work if you can. Talk to teachers about transferring classes, moving your locker, or needing to work off-site for a week or two until things calm down. You could also change your phone number if you feel that blocking your ex's number isn't going to be enough.

- If you are worried about them turning up at your home, arrange to stay somewhere else for a while. This should be with someone they don't know, if possible, rather than your best friend (an obvious choice). Make sure you have all the resources you need, including money for bus fare, school books, clothes, phone and charger, laptop, etc.

- If you have text messages or voicemails that are threatening or show emotional blackmail, store a copy of them on a drive, take screenshots, or print them out. Take photos of any bruises or injuries your partner gave you, and make a note in a journal of times they have been intimidating, and also of any conversations you have had with adults about your concerns. No teen should be having to do this, but in extreme cases, you might want this evidence to back up requests to school or for police reports.

- You can't, and shouldn't, do this alone. Tell trusted adults what you are afraid of, what has already happened, and what you plan to do. Ask for their help and advice and let them support you. You've probably been feeling isolated and afraid that no one will believe you or care about what is happening, and finding out that other people do can give you the strength to move on.

  - Trusted adults include school staff, religious leaders, adults from sports clubs, family members, friends' parents, adult siblings, social workers, and the police. Of course, you can tell your friends as well; maybe it's easier to open up to them first and have them help you to tell an adult, but don't rely on just your friends to help you through this. They don't have the experience or the resources that adults have, and you don't want to risk your friends' safety as well.

## How to Break up With an Abuser

Plan what you want to say in advance. You could even write it all down if you know you're going to do it over the phone or by message. Having a script can make you feel more confident, and you will know that you won't leave anything out or start babbling.

Keep it short. There's no need to go into great detail about anything or say something that might anger them. State clearly that you are breaking up with them and the relationship has now ended. Tell them that you were not happy, and include information about why if you are comfortable. Make it very clear that you do not want to be friends and they are not to contact you again. Then hang up, or leave.

You do not owe them the chance to respond or to say their piece. You do not owe them any explanation or promise of further contact. If you have any of their stuff that you know they're going to want back, bring it with you or arrange for a friend or trusted adult to return it on your behalf.

## Afterthoughts

Ending a relationship can be difficult under any circum-stances, and you might find yourself feeling sad, de-pressed, or worried that you did the wrong thing. It's important to be honest with your support team about your feelings so that they can help you process them and start to move forward. If you find that too difficult, you should consider talking to a counselor or a healthcare professional. They will be able to suggest some therapies or medication to help you feel more like yourself again.

# Chapter Eight

---

# Dating: Not Just for Cishets

*W̲E̲ ̲D̲E̲S̲E̲R̲V̲E̲ ̲T̲O̲ ̲E̲X̲P̲E̲R̲I̲E̲N̲C̲E̲ love fully, equally, without shame and without compromise.* –Elliot Page

Your teenage years are times of great change, both internally and externally. Your brain is rewiring itself, your body is developing its adult shape, and your reproductive system kicks in, opening a whole new world of attraction, dating, and sex. It's a time to explore your options, try new things, and discover what makes you, well, you! That includes unraveling all these new feelings you're (possibly) having toward other people, and working out your sexuality, and maybe even your gender.

## A Time for Exploration

Dating can be daunting enough if you're cisgender and straight, but at least then you're in the majority. You're more likely to find information relating to your experiences and see yourself reflected in the media. If you don't feel like you fall into this box, there's no rush to put a label on your feelings, and if you do, don't worry if you want to change it at a later date. Some adults take years to decide that they fall onto the LGBT+ spectrum and where exactly they land, so take your time and just enjoy the experience of experimenting and exploring your sexuality. You might find that dating a wide range of people over your teenage years will help you figure out what you feel. Alternatively, you might not want to date anyone until you have sorted everything out in your own head. There's no "right" way to go about it; only the right way for you.

Our understanding of different sexualities has grown a lot in recent years. Most people would accept that people are no longer just "gay" or "straight," but that there is a whole range of ways to experience love. Asexual (ace) and aromantic (aro) people feel little or no sexual or romantic attraction toward others, but that doesn't stop them from forming loving relationships with others who share or accept their boundaries. People who identify as bisexual or pansexual find themselves romantically and/or sexually attracted to people of more than one gender, while homosexuals are attracted to people whose gender matches theirs. Heterosexual men are at-tracted to women and women are attracted to men.

LGBT+ dating might feel harder because you know fewer people going through the same thing, but in reality, you and the cishets are all feeling the same worries. Will my crush like me? What should I wear on a first date? How do I ask if I can kiss them? If you want to find other LGBT+ people to talk to about dating, attraction, and figuring everything out, you can look online for established communities in your country. This is probably the best way to find people who have been through it all and who can guide you, as well as others who are asking the same questions about themselves.

## How to Make LGBT+ Dating Comfortable

If you've decided that you want to start dating, and you identify as LGBT+, you might face a few extra obstacles than your cishet friends. For a start, your potential dating pool is likely a lot smaller, so finding someone you are attracted to who will also be attracted to you can be difficult, and this is understandably frustrating. Again, searching for an online community, or a local LGBT+ group can help to put you in touch with other LGBT+ teenagers, so you can start to build a network of friends, supporters, and eventually, prospective partners. Bear in mind that not all LGBT+ teens in your area will be out at school or in the community, so you might think that you're alone, but find some surprising new friends.

You don't need to be out to be dating, and neither does your partner, but you do need to be willing and able to talk to each other about what this means. You might be out to your friends, only a few people, or no one at all, and they need to respect your decision and not do anything to compromise this. It can be hard, keeping yet another secret (your relationship) on top of everything else, but ultimately you both need to move at your own speeds.

This might mean that you go on a lot of dates with groups of friends so that, to outsiders, they don't look like dates at all. Secretly holding hands at the movies can feel so much more exciting and intimate than the public displays your straight friends make, and these special moments can make the bond between the two of you much stronger. If at least one of you is out at home, then you have a great safe space in which to enjoy each other's company. Netflix marathons are your new best friend and there's no need to go out when you can stay in.

## Embrace the Community

Being part of the LGBT+ community can have some pretty awesome benefits you might not have thought of. There's so much competition between cishets—friends fancying the same person, feeling like they need to have the most attractive partner, or not be single for too long—and society heaps more pressure for them to conform to the images put out there by the media.

There are fewer expectations for LGBT+ teens about what their partner should look like, when they should start dating, and how fast those relationships should move. In fact, if anything, you're expected to date less, date later, and date slower than your peers. It may not seem like much, but trust me, dating without worrying that other people think you're "behind" is a liberating experience. Of course, if you're not out, you will still get the same questions from relatives about when you're going to get a partner, but you'll just have to chalk that up to normal dating problems!

You're far less likely to be crushing on the same person as your friends (of the same gender anyway).  Nothing kills a friendship faster than finding out you both like the same person, especially if one of you ends up dating them. In high school, I had a friend who was harboring secret feelings for her best friend. When he started dating her younger sister, all hell broke loose and the two girls couldn't be in the same room as each other for weeks. It made car rides to school very awkward!

Having to set so many boundaries and be careful about who you tell what to is going to give you both excellent communication skills. You're going to be so good at talking about your needs and listening to those of your partner that all your cishet friends are going to think you're some sort of relationship magician. You're also going to be in the uniquely special position of being able to understand a lot more of what your partner is going through and how they feel. I'm way past my teenage years and I still find myself baffled sometimes by the way that women think and some of the things that they do, and I know my female friends feel the same about their male partners. Having a history of shared experiences, even if some of them are negative, gives you a stronger bond.

## Looking for That Special Someone

Finding your perfect partner may not be as simple for you as your cishet friends, but they will be out there somewhere. I've already mentioned the internet as a great place to find people to talk to, and there's nothing to say you can't also find an online, long-distance, or even reasonably-local partner. Whether you do or don't, having a safe space where you can talk with people who understand you and who have been in your shoes is invaluable.

In the UK, visit theproudtrust.org to find local LGBT+ groups in your area where you can meet up and socialize with other LGBT+ teenagers. They also have information about online groups and specific groups for trans teens and YPoC teens.

In the US, pflag.org will help you find a local chapter. With regular meetings and events all over the country, they will be able to support you and offer advice and a safe space to be yourself.

Internationally, trevorspace.org offers a teens-only chat space and forum where you can set your own identity, get advice from your peers, and find thousands of people just like you.

# Chapter Nine

## **The Practical Stuff**

*I THINK I HAVE a problem. My body has complete control over me.* –Otis Milburn

We can't talk about teenage dating without addressing the elephant in the room; at some point or another, the topic of sex is going to come up. For such a universal human experience, the way in which people talk about it is hugely varied. Some cultures—especially in Scandinavian countries—are very open about sex and happy to discuss it in a way that is practical and helpful and removes any sense of shame or worry that teens might have about broaching the subject. Other cultures prefer to treat any discussion of sex as a massive taboo, often leading to a lot of misinformation spreading among those who are curious. It's perfectly natural that you would have questions about something you've never done before, especially when sex isn't often viewed as an optional activity. Imagine if you got to your 16th birthday and were suddenly handed a basketball and told you were playing in a game that evening, despite not knowing the rules and having never trained or practiced a day in your life. Sounds terrifying to me.

So, in order to try and counter some of the dodgy advice and information that tends to be found online or passed around the school corridors, here's a brief look at how to incorporate physical intimacy into your relationships, and what exactly that might look like.

## The Many Faces of Physical Intimacy

One of the things that can set a romantic relationship apart from a platonic one is that you have more physical contact. When someone you feel close to touches you, your brain releases oxytocin (which makes you feel warm and fuzzy inside) and serotonin (which makes you feel happier), and this makes you want to spend more time with them (Good Clean Love, 2021). Touch works both ways too; when you put your hand on your partner's shoulder, you both get the benefits of the contact, which is why you not only enjoy being touched by your partner but also want to reach out and touch them too.

The ways in which you and your partner can enjoy physical intimacy will depend on a number of things, including

131

how old you both are, how long you have been together, and your personal comfort levels. It's worth highlighting that not everyone responds to touch in the same way. Some people find the thought of hugging or touching someone else makes them uncomfortable. This doesn't have to come from a place of trauma or bad experience; it's just that different people process sensations in different ways. This is why setting physical boundaries at the beginning of a relationship is really important.

## Sexual Intimacy

As you grow older and go through puberty, you might become more interested in sex. For some people, who may then identify as asexual, sex doesn't always become a factor in their relationships, but for many others, sexual intimacy becomes desirable as you grow closer to your partner. But just because you're in a relationship, and you're both over the age of consent, that doesn't mean you need to jump straight into having sex. If neither of you is ready, or you're both younger, there are plenty of ways you can enjoy each other's touch without involving penetration. Here's a brief rundown of some of the ways you and your partner could be physically and sexually intimate:

- Kissing. Not every kiss belongs in a romantic movie, and you don't have to use your tongue to inspect your partner's cavities. Kisses on the cheek, head, shoulder, and hand are often the most intimate.

- Cuddling. From big bear hugs to an arm around the waist, or snuggling together on the couch with legs and arms intertwined, cuddling with your partner is a great way to feel closer together, both literally and emotionally.

- Holding hands. Often one of the sweetest intimate gestures because it's a subtle but public signal that the two of you are a couple. It can also be a way of staying connected or showing solidarity, or if you aren't out as a couple yet, held hands can be hidden under a table to turn this gesture from public to private.

- Making out. This is the one that starts getting your pulse racing. Deep kisses, or kissing sensual places such as the neck or collar bones, combined with touching the hips, waist, and chest. Best not to have your make-out session anywhere public, even though you usually keep your clothes on.

- Mutual masturbation. Masturbation, whatever you might hear to the contrary, is such a natural activity that a surprising amount of the animal kingdom is at it, including most primates, dolphins, squirrels, and even penguins. It not only releases more happy hormones in your brain, but it can also relieve stress and act as a pain killer! It's a really good way of getting to know your own body and what you like, meaning when you are ready to have sexual contact with a partner, you can guide them to make it a pleasurable experience for you. Mutual masturbation involves masturbating with your partner. Some people like to combine this with kissing and making out, but the end result is that you both touch yourselves.

So far, this list hasn't included any contact where you are touching each other directly in intimate areas, but that's about to change. Make sure that both you and your partner are 100% comfortable with anything else on this list before proceeding. Remember to get, and give, explicit consent for all activities, and it's a good idea to discuss any boundaries beforehand. For example, if you are happy with being touched under your clothes, but you're not ready for your partner to see you naked, you can arrange to keep your clothes on or stay under a sheet.

- Sexual touching is a similar activity to mutual masturbation, except this time you are touching each other. Remember to be gentle with your partner, especially when touching delicate areas. Don't be afraid to give instructions, or ask for them. If this is your first time with your partner, even if you have experience with other partners beforehand, you should remember that everyone likes different things, and it's very unlikely you will magically hit all the right buttons on the first try.

- Oral sex. Remember, if you are going to ask anyone to put their mouth anywhere near your genitals, give them a good clean first! It's common sense and makes it a more pleasant experience for your partner. Oral sex involves you stimulating your partner with your mouth, lips, and tongue. This means licking, sucking, and kissing their penis or vulva until they have an orgasm or as part of foreplay before penetrative sex.

- Anal sex. Again, cleanliness is important, so make sure you clean your anus beforehand and that everyone cleans their hands afterward. This is so important if you are going to be touching other areas, as you can end up transferring bacteria and fecal matter, which could then cause an infection. Anal sex involves inserting a finger, penis, or dildo into the anal cavity and can be enjoyed by all sexes if done carefully. Unlike the vagina, your anus doesn't produce its own lubrication, so you will need to buy some lube and use it liberally. Anal sex is not something that everyone feels like trying, so don't be offended if your partner re-fuses a request, and don't be afraid to turn them down if it's not something that you want to do.

- Penetrative vaginal sex, where a penis or dildo is inserted into a vagina—which makes it sound much less fun and intimate than it really is. When aroused, the vagina secretes a clear lubricant, the muscles relax, and more blood flows to the area, increasing the sensitivity of the nerve endings. Stimulating these can be pleasurable; although, often other touching, like rubbing of the clitoris, is needed to have an orgasm. Each person is dif-ferent.

## When There's Conflict

Where sex is concerned, there isn't really a "usual" or "normal" in terms of how to approach it in a relationship. For some people, the decision to get sexually intimate with another is a big deal that they take their time over; for others, it isn't. Some people are comfortable with sexual contact early in a relationship; others want to keep all physical exploration off the table until they are married. You and your partner might have the same expectations—if you met through a church youth group, for example—or you might be coming from very different places. This is why communication and respect are key.

This might also be the only time when I don't advocate compromise. If you and your partner have different opinions about what you want to do with your body, you should not have to step out of your comfortable place to make them happy, and vice versa. Here's an example:

Todd (17) and Becca (18) met at a basketball club and started dating after a few weeks. They have been out to the movies a couple of times with friends and then to a club party, where they had their first kiss at the end of the night. Becca texted Todd afterward with a few flirty suggestions that hinted that she would be up for more than kissing next time. Todd calls Becky the next day and suggests they meet for a coffee to talk about some things. When they do, he tells her that he isn't ready for a physical relationship beyond kissing and cuddling. He had always thought that he would wait until he was married, or at least well into a serious relationship. Becca isn't a virgin and in her previous relationship, she enjoyed the sexual connection alongside the emotional one. What should they do?

A compromise is designed to find a middle ground between two options, but here that would mean asking Todd to cross his boundary. Instead, it is Becca who needs to decide if she's ready to compromise on her expectations. She should respect Todd's opinion, and either commit to a relationship that would be missing an aspect she would otherwise like, or she should step away and find someone who she can be sexually close to if that is what is important to her.

Another point of conflict can come between what you want to do and your own body. Don't forget that attraction and arousal are biological processes that will happen regardless of whether you want them to or not. (Sometimes they don't happen when you desperately wish they would, especially when you get older, but that's a problem for another time!) It can be really frustrating when your body is trying to lead you down the physical path but you want to wait. Try to remember that it's just a reaction—like pulling your hand away if you touch something hot, or salivating when you smell dinner cooking—and it doesn't mean that you have to follow through with anything that you aren't emotionally ready for. And, if you find it all gets too much, that's when masturbation can come in handy!

## Safe Sex: Why, When, and How

If you and your partner are both wanting to have a sexual relationship and have both given your explicit consent, then you need to be mature about it. At the end of the day, there are added responsibilities that come with sex—after all, its primary biological function is reproduction, not pleasure. You should discuss what you would both do in the event of an unplanned pregnancy and consider whether you are both ready to deal with the consequences.

When we talk about having safe sex, there are two main reasons: to prevent unwanted pregnancies and to protect against the spread of sexually transmitted diseases (STDs). The best way to avoid either is to abstain from sexual contact with other people, but that's also a bit like saying you won't catch the flu if you lock yourself in your house all day. If you are going to engage in a sexual relationship, you need to know how to keep yourself and your partner safe.

## Contraceptive Options

Contraceptives are designed to dramatically reduce the risk of pregnancy. Many also protect against the transmission of STDs, but not all. It's very common nowadays for young women to be prescribed a contraceptive pill, but this offers no protection against STDs and should be used in partnership with a barrier method like the male or female condom or a diaphragm. You can make an appointment with your doctor, school nurse, or at a local sexual health clinic if you want to discuss your choices. They will give you all the facts and help you to decide which methods will work best for you.

Generally, contraceptives are split into two options: barrier and hormonal. At the moment, hormonal contraceptives are only available for the female reproductive system. Hormonal contraceptives work by releasing hormones that interrupt the body's natural cycle, meaning that the ovaries don't release an egg, or the cervix doesn't thin to let sperm through. Contraceptive pills need to be taken every day to be reliable, while implants or injections are longer lasting. The less the contraceptive has to rely on a human to work (fitting condoms correctly, taking the pill regularly), the more effective it is, so long-lasting hormonal contraceptives can be around 99% effective at preventing pregnancy (NHS Choices, 2019). However, they don't protect against STDs.

Barrier contraceptives do protect against infections, but they can be less effective than contraceptives because they are more fiddly. Putting a condom on or the diaphragm in wrong can reduce its effectiveness by 10–20% (NHS Choices, 2019). It's worth practicing by yourself to make sure that you feel confident before you end up trying to fit one during a romantic encounter.

It's really good practice to always use condoms when you start to have sex with a new partner. This will protect you from pregnancies and STDs. Remember, both partners are responsible for their sexual safety, so don't assume that you won't need any contraceptives because you think your partner has it covered. Are you willing and able to look after a baby or deal with an incurable STD? No, so it's your responsibility to make sure you don't end up with any unwanted surprises. Hormonal and barrier contraceptives can be used together to increase your protection against both pregnancy and STDs, so don't worry about doubling up.

## No Glove, No Love

Most STDs are transmitted through skin-to-skin contact, or the exchange of bodily fluids including blood, semen, saliva, and vaginal lubricant. You only need one exposure to become infected, and there doesn't need to have been penetrative sex involved. If there are traces of semen on your fingers and you touch them to your mouth or to a vagina, the infection can be passed on.

The best way to protect yourself is to regularly get tested, and insist that your partner does too. If you're both in a committed relationship where you're only having sexual contact with each other, and you both have a clean bill of health, then there's no chance of catching an STD. It's a sensible practice to both get tested at the start of each new sexual relationship. One of the main reasons that STDs spread so rapidly is because many of them don't have any obvious symptoms, so you could easily not know that you have one. However, this doesn't mean that they're harmless, as some can cause infertility while others cause liver damage, increase your chances of developing cancer, or weaken your immune system.

Some common STDs are easily treatable while others can be long-lasting. Chlamydia, gonorrhea, syphilis, and trichomoniasis all respond well to antibiotics, so all you need to do is complete the course and stay away from sexual activity until you're given the all-clear. However, due to the increased use of antibiotics, there are a number of strains of gonorrhea that are becoming resistant and making treatment harder. Other STDs like herpes, hepatitis B, and HIV currently have no cure, but they can be kept under control with anti-viral medication (World Health Organization, 2022).

## What if Accidents Happen?

Other than abstaining from all forms of sexual contact, there is no contraceptive that is 100% effective, but many have less than a 1% chance of failure if they are used correctly. Combining a barrier method and a hormonal method will drastically reduce this chance of failure while also protecting you against STDs. But even so, sometimes accidents happen. Condoms can break, medications (including some antibiotics) can make the pill less effective, and drinking alcohol or being stressed or unwell can mean you forget to take one.

If you notice that your barrier contraceptive has failed, you can get emergency contraceptives from your local sexual health center, like Planned Parenthood or Marie

Stopes, or from your pharmacy. You don't need a pre-scription, but it is often free or has a small charge. You should also arrange an STD test just to be safe.

It is less obvious when hormonal contraceptives have failed and couples often don't realize until noticing early pregnancy symptoms such as a missed period, swollen breasts, nausea, and bloating. You should book an ap-pointment with your local healthcare provider or sexual health clinic as soon as possible to discuss your options.

Abortions are not legal everywhere, so be aware that if this is the right solution for you, you may need help trav-eling to a safe location. You will need supportive people with you because this is an emotional experience, even for adults.

If you choose to continue with the pregnancy, you have the choice to keep your baby or arrange an adoption. Only you know what is the right solution for you, but it is still important to discuss your options with a supportive and trusted adult. You do not have to go through the experience alone.

# Chapter Ten

---

# When it Doesn't Work Out

*T*AKE YOUR BROKEN HEART, *make it into art.* –Carrie Fisher

Unlike a number of other books on the market, I'm not going to promise you that reading mine will guarantee you a date. People are still people after all, with their own wants, likes, and desires. It doesn't matter how nicely you ask someone out; if they don't fancy you, they aren't going to say yes. And if they feel like they have to, even though they don't want to, that's not going to lead to a very fun date, is it?

Rejection and heartbreak are unpleasant, but they teach you how to move on. This is a vital skill that will make you a more stable and adaptable adult. Leaving school, leaving university, changing friendship groups, failing an interview, being fired from a job: These are all instances of rejection and upset that most of you will have to face in the future, why should the ending of a relationship make you feel any worse? Just because the media projects an image of heartbreak that involved binging on ice cream and sobbing into your pillow, doesn't mean every ending needs to be sad.

## Rejection Isn't the End of the World

There can be a number of reasons why asking someone out ends in a rejection, and here's the important thing to remember:

**All of them are valid.**

- They just don't fancy you. Sorry, but you're not everyone's type, and as much as it might hurt when someone you really like doesn't feel the same way, it's a pretty common occurrence.

- They're seeing someone already. Maybe you just didn't know, or maybe no one knows, but at least you can't take this one personally.

- They don't want to date anyone. Not everyone is ready for the experience, and you should respect them for having the courage to be different.

- They're still figuring out their sexual or gender identity. With so much going on, they might not have the emotional capacity to form any new relationships, or you might be entirely not their type.

- Their family, culture, or religion forbids them from dating. Their existing relationships with their family and background aren't worth sacrificing for a date or two, no matter how many movies you've seen with a similar plot.

If someone turns you down, be polite about it. They have made a decision, for whatever reason, and they don't owe you an explanation or another chance. I'm sure you would want to be treated the same way. Believe me, they aren't suddenly going to change their mind because you start pleading, shouting, negging, or anything else other than walking away.

## Breakups Are a Part of Life

The number of people worldwide who end up marrying their high school sweetheart is minuscule. More than 99% of you will experience at least one romantic relationship ending, either by your hand, theirs, or as a victim of circumstance.

## Welcome to Dumpsville, Population: Them

The less involved and committed the relationship has become, the easier it should be to break things off. If, after a couple of dates, you don't think that you're a compatible pair, a quick polite text is usually enough to end things. For example:

*Hi. I had a great time last time we went out, but the more I see you, the more I realize there isn't really a spark. Sorry, but I don't think we should do it again. I hope you understand.*

Once you've passed the dating stage and officially declared yourself a couple, you at least owe the other person a face-to-face conversation. Unless you're concerned about putting yourself in danger, in which case, all manners can go out the window.

Tell your partner that you want to talk about your relationship and give them a time and place for the chat. Don't lead them to believe you're going on another date; they will feel ambushed and that will make them act defensively. You have two choices: Calmly explain that you don't think things are working between you (you can explain why if you want to be specific) and either say you would like to end the relationship or discuss ways in which you can work together to improve it.

However, don't be talked into staying together if you are set on parting ways. This will twist the relationship into unhealthy territory and they will become dependent on you. It's reasonable to expect your partner to become emotional, so be prepared for some resistance, but ultimately, if one person doesn't want to be in a relationship, there isn't a relationship to save.

## Population: You

You might now know how to be a decent human being and break up with someone as gently as you can, but not everyone will be as respectful. Often you can tell when the end is coming, but other times you'll feel like being dumped came out of the blue. The hardest part is often respecting your partner's (now, ex-partner's) decision, but it's really important. Hopefully, they will offer you an explanation so that you can get some closure. If it was something you did that they didn't click with, you can learn from the situation, but most often it's probably not one thing that ended the relationship. Remember, once that initial passion fizzles out, many people realize that they don't actually have that much in common, or even like spending that much time together!

## Putting Yourself Back Together

When a relationship ends, you are allowed to take time to mourn it. After all, it was a significant relationship in your life for a period of time, and now it's gone. You can't share the same in-jokes with your friends or rely on the same hug when you're having a bad day. It takes time to readjust to a new normal. But you will have friends who can rally around and help pick you up, as well as family, school work, hobbies, or a part-time job—all of which will provide a welcome distraction.

While it's natural to want to hide away and feel sad, eventually you will need to re-emerge into the world. Here are some ways you can start to heal:

- Avoid your ex as much as you can. If you have the same friends, this can be difficult, but explain to them that you need space from your ex and ask that they arrange things separately with each of you for a while.

- Rediscover something you love doing that you haven't had time for recently. Maybe your ex didn't like superhero movies, so you've got a backlog of Marvel films to catch up on, or the stack of books waiting to be read is piling up on your shelves. Do something that is just for you and enjoy it.

- It's okay to feel lonely now, but that doesn't mean you have to be alone. Organize things with your

149

friends, say yes to parties, or even try hanging out with your annoying little sister. Spending time with people who appreciate you will help you remember that you're awesome and you don't need a relationship to make you interesting.

- Look after yourself physically. Make sure you're eating well and getting enough sleep. Now that you have a bit of time for yourself, why not try a new activity like yoga or running, or join a softball or soccer team?

Once you have a bit of distance from your relationship, you can look back and see what you can learn from it. Every finished relationship teaches you a little more about yourself; what you like or dislike, how much space you need, and whether you rush heart-first into everything and could do with a slightly slower approach. Next time, you will be a little wiser about what mistakes to avoid and what you need to ask for, which should lead to a happier, healthier, and possibly more successful partnership.

## Unhelpful Behaviors

Sometimes, what you feel like doing and what you should be doing are two very different things. It can take maturity to recognize unhealthy behaviors, but here are a few to help you on your way. If you find yourself doing these after a breakup, try and make the switch to something healthier instead.

- Stalking your ex on social media or asking friends what they're up to. Unfollow and block them on social media and don't be tempted to keep checking back. In fact, it would be healthy to take a break from social media for a week or two and focus on yourself, instead of looking at photos of other people looking happy.

- Don't binge eat for longer than a day or two. If you eat too much junk food, drink alcohol, and stay up all night, you're going to end up feeling like crap. You won't feel better emotionally unless you also feel good physically, so push yourself to get some exercise and give yourself a mood boost.

- There's no point pining for your ex or your relationship; both are gone now. Yes, you can—and should—let yourself feel sad about it, but if it goes on for longer than a couple of weeks, you should see your doctor and talk about getting some counseling or trying antidepressants to help you get back on top of your emotions.

If the problem isn't you but your ex, then you might want to consider involving a trusted adult. They shouldn't be messaging you or turning up at your locker, team meet, or house, and this is a form of harassment. Don't be afraid to tell them to stop or report their behavior to the school, their parents, or even the police. If they're making you feel unsafe, they need to stop.

# Conclusion

You'll notice that some of your peers make dating look effortless. They're always coupled up and loved up and never seem to have worries. Others will shrivel at the thought of having to ask someone out, preferring to dote on them from afar and imagining endless scenarios where they aren't feeling so socially awkward. Where you fall on that scale will probably change slightly from day to day, but wherever that is, don't ever worry that you aren't having a normal experience.

There are a multitude of reasons why you might feel awkward about entering the dating game:

- Low self-esteem and poor body image can convince you that no one will ever find you attractive, and by building up your confidence and finding ways to feel good about yourself, you'll come to love yourself, and that will make you more attractive to others than any haircut, makeup, or fancy clothing.

- Having a tiny circle of friends, living in a small town, or not having opportunities to meet other teens can make you feel like you'll never be able to meet someone special. But by seeking out new hobbies and interests, utilizing the internet to carefully make more contacts, and generally putting yourself out there more, you will soon realize that your social circle is wider than you thought. And who knows; maybe the next person you meet will steal your heart.

- If your identity doesn't fall neatly into the cishet bracket, it's easy to feel that your dating options are more limited. You're dealing with a lot more than most other teens, so be kind to yourself and don't force anything to happen. Find yourself an amazing support network and spend time with other LGBT+ young people to build your community, get comfortable in your own skin, and you will eventually attract someone who loves you for exactly who you are.

Never mind what images the media and the internet put out there; it's entirely your choice whether your want to date or not, and whether you want to enjoy a healthy, age-appropriate physical relationship or wait until you are older or married. There's no ideal "right" time to be dating, and you won't gain any benefits or suffer any hardships from starting earlier or later than your peers.

In fact, the "right" time to start dating is going to be different for everyone, and most often it is when you find someone that you are attracted to. Hopefully, they are going to be attracted to you too, but if not, remember that rejection is nothing to be ashamed of. It doesn't mean you did anything wrong, or that there is anything wrong with you, all it means is that you and that person weren't the right fit. After all, I'm sure you can name some kids you know that you don't want to be friends with because you know you'd have very little in common to talk about or do together.

Romantic relationships are just like any other; you can't force them. They grow and blossom when two people with common interests, experiences, and values come together and are ignited by a little spark of attraction. But like most other social interactions in your life, people won't necessarily be drawn to you if you don't feel confident and content in your own skin. By building a great relationship with yourself first, others will be able to see all your best qualities, and your little spark will become a bright flame.

*"Thank you for completing this book. If you've enjoyed it, please consider leaving an honest review on your Amazon store, which will be most helpful to others.*
*Thank you,*
*Kev"*

**Teens' Guide to Dating**

Click here

**Teens' Guide to Dating**

Click here

## Teens' Guide Series

### Teens' Guide to Making Friends

Click

Teens' Guide to Making Friends

### Teens' Guide to Health and Mental Wellness

Click

Teens' Guide to Health and Mental Wellness

## FREEBIES

(Click book covers to access)

GROWN UP'S GUIDE TO

# COMMUNICATING
# WITH TEENS

BUILDING TRUST, STRENGTHENING BONDS A PARENT'S
GUIDE TO EFFECTIVE TEEN COMMUNICATION

KEV CHILTON

# About the Author

Having a stark choice of fighting teens on the city streets or helping them find their way in life, Kev Chilton knew which way he wanted to go!

For most of his working life, he was an inner-city cop and detective, concentrating on murder, gun crime, and other serious offences.

However, he joined the police as a 16-year-old cadet and early in his career, he was tasked with helping young offenders, which quickly became his speciality. He noticed that by simply listening to the problems young people were concerned with, the majority were prepared to listen to him back. He built trusting relationships with most, who were happy to listen to and act on his advice. Many responded positively, and they moved confidently into adulthood.

Throughout his police service, he arranged youth clubs, attended schools where he gave talks and maintained an open-door policy, encouraging any young person with a problem to approach him privately afterwards. He also set up and operated specialist juvenile squads geared towards helping those who had gone off the rails. The results were excellent, and he was never happier in his job than when he could redirect a young person's life onto the right path.

It was a fulfilling time in his life, and it helped him understand the constantly evolving challenges teenagers face as they transition to adulthood. More specifically, as times change, so do the needs and circumstances of young people. Choosing the path of mentorship over the chaos of city streets, he has dedicated his journey to helping teenagers, steering them away from conflict and towards a brighter future.

Through a series of empowering 'How-to' guidebooks for teens, Chilton has become a beacon of support for them.

Today, he is proud to utilise his extensive experience to make a positive impact. He is particularly attuned to the unique issues that young people are currently grappling with, and one of his goals is to bridge the gap between them and the adults in their lives.

He lives in a cold barn out in the country where he constantly fights the elements—a losing battle that keeps him off the streets!

To chat with the author and to find more information about the community he is building, visit his website at:

**Teens' Guide Series Website**

Website

Click here

Join the Teens' Guide Series mailing list and connect with our friendly community, get up-to-date information and details of further book launches in this five-book series.

**Teens' Guide Series Mailing List**

Mailing List

Click here

# Dedication

With special thanks to Beth, whose initial conversations guided my journey to create this five-book series.

Also, a special thanks to Grace for her meticulous research and invaluable advice, which played a pivotal role in creating the final product.

And to my good friend, Anna, who kept me sane throughout!

# References

ABRAHAM, R. (2021, SEPTEMBER 30). *Why is Confidence Attractive*. LinkedIn https://www.linkedin.com/pulse/why-confidence-attractive-dr-reza-abraham

Alliance, N. C. (2018, March 15). *7 Rules Your Teens Should Follow While Online Dating*. National Cybersecurity Alliance. https://staysafeonline.org/online-safety-privacy-basics/7-rules-teens-follow-online-dating/

Andersen, C. H. (2021, February 16). *17 Relationship Communication Quotes Every Couple Will Love*. The Healthy. https://www.thehealthy.com/family/relationships/relationship-communication-quotes/

Ayer, R. (2019, September 6). *Teens who don't date are less depressed and have better social skills*. ScienceDaily. https://www.sciencedaily.com/releases/2019/09/190906134007.htm

BBC Bitesize. (2019, October 4). *The psychology of attrac-tion: Why do we fancy certain people?* https://www.bbc.c o.uk/bitesize/articles/zm9ry9q

Better Help. (2023, May 30). *22 Body Lan-guage Examples And What They Show | Better-help.* https://www.betterhelp.com/advice/body-languag e/22-body-language-examples-and-what-they-show/

Calkins, I., & Lopez, V. (2023, April 24). *30 Breakup Texts to Send That Are Way Nicer Than Ghosting.* Cos-mopolitan. https://www.cosmopolitan.com/sex-love/a2 8638581/breakup-texts/

Cherry, K. (2021, December 1). *6 Different Types of Relationships You May Find Yourself In.* Verywell Mind. https://www.verywellmind.com/6-types-of-relati onships-and-their-effect-on-your-life-5209431

Chrysalis Courses. (2019). *Why communication is key to re-lationships.* https://www.chrysaliscourses.ac.uk/news/w hy-communication-is-key-to-healthy-relationships

Commonwealth of Massachusetts. (n.d.). *Recognizing the signs of unhealthy relationships | Mass.gov.* Www.mass .gov. https://www.mass.gov/service-details/recognizing -the-signs-of-unhealthy-relationships

Good Clean Love. (2021, March 19). *The Sci-ence of Intimate Touching: Why We Need*

*It*. https://goodcleanlove.com/blogs/making-love-sustai nable/the-science-of-intimate-touching-why-we-need-it

Goodreads. (n.d.). *Consent Quotes (145 quotes)*. https://w ww.goodreads.com/quotes/tag/consent

Headspace. (2022, September 14). *How To Get Over A Relationship Breakup | Head- space*. https://headspace.org.au/explore-topics/for-you ng-people/relationship-breakup/

Homeschool and Humor. (2022, September 9). *100 Beautiful Self-Confidence Quotes for Girls And Teens*. https://www.homeschoolandhumor.com/self-co nfidence-quotes-for-girls-and-teens/

Kirby, S. (2022, August 12). *Sex Education Quotes From The Teen Comedy and Drama Series*. Everyday Power. https:/ /everydaypower.com/sex-education-quotes/

LeDuc, M. (2021, December 23). *Talking to LGBTQ+ Teens About Sex and Relationships | Power to Decide*. Powerto decide.org. https://powertodecide.org/news/talking-lgb tq-teens-about-sex-and-relationships

Love is Respect. (n.d.). *Dating in the closet*. https://www. loveisrespect.org/resources/dating-in-the-closet/

Mind. (2022, August). *Tips to improve your self-esteem | Mind, the mental health charity - help for mental health problems*. Mind.org.uk.

https://www.mind.org.uk/information-support/types-of
-mental-health-problems/self-esteem/tips-to-improve-y
our-self-esteem/

Myers, E. (2022, January 31). *Sternberg's Triangular Theory and the 8 Types of Love | Simply Psychology*. Www.simp lypsychology.org. https://www.simplypsychology.org/ty pes-of-love-we-experience.html

Nemours. (n.d.). *STDs (Sexually Transmitted Diseases) (for Teens) - Nemours KidsHealth*. Kidshealth.org. https://kids health.org/en/teens/std.html

NHS Choices. (2019). *Your contraception guide*. NHS. https://www.nhs.uk/conditions/contraception/ho w-effective-contraception/

Parenting Teens and Tweens. (2022, April 5). *More Than 30 Positive Affirmations For Your Teen To Help Their Confidence and Mental Health*. https://parentingteensandtweens.com/more-than-30-p ositive-affirmations-for-your-teen-to-help-their-confiden ce-and-mental-health/

PFlag. (n.d.). *Find a Chapter*. PFLAG. https://pflag.org/fin dachapter/

Planned Parenthood. (n.d.). *Relationship Communication Skills For Teenagers*. https://www.plannedparenthood.o rg/learn/teens/relationships/all-about-communication

Poitevien, J. (2021, January 28). *Are Intimate Friend-ships and Romantic Relationships Different at All?* Well+Good. https://www.wellandgood.com/differences-between-friendship-romance/

Raising Children Network. (2021, April 23). *Brain development in pre-teens and teenagers*. Raising Children Network. https://raisingchildren.net.au/pre-teens/development/understanding-your-pre-teen/brain-development-teens

Rothman, E. (2023, January 10). *Talking with Teens and Preteens About Pornography | Common Sense Media*. Www.commonsensemedia.org. https://www.commonsensemedia.org/articles/talking-with-teens-and-preteens-about-pornography

Safer Schools. (2021, October 29). *Incels in the Classroom: The Worrying Rise of an Online Subculture*. https://oursaferschools.co.uk/2021/10/29/incels/

Sager, J. (2021, June 10). *50 LGBTQ Quotes to Celebrate Pride Month, Encourage Equality and Remind Us All that Love Is Love*. Parade: Entertainment, Recipes, Health, Life, Holidays. https://parade.com/1221493/jessicasager/lgbtq-quotes/

Sarah. (2019, June 21). *7 Simple Ways To Stay Safe On A Date*. Tailor Matched. https://tailormatched.com/7-simple-ways-to-stay-safe-on-a-date/

Scott, E. (2022, January 25). *How to Improve Your Relationships With Effective Communication Skills*. Verywell Mind. https://www.verywellmind.com/managing-conflict-in-relationships-communication-tips-3144967

Sorensen, S. (2007). *Adolescent Romantic Relationships*. https://www.dibbleinstitute.org/Documents/reasearch_facts_romantic_0707.pdf

Stonewall. (2020, May 28). *List of LGBTQ+ terms*. Stonewall. https://www.stonewall.org.uk/list-lgbtq-terms

Sweet, N. (n.d.). *Navigating gay relationships in high school*. The Record. https://record.horacemann.org/4112/features/navigating-gay-relationships-in-high-school/

The Jed Foundation. (n.d.). *How to safely end an unhealthy relationship | JED*. https://jedfoundation.org/resource/how-to-safely-end-unhealthy-relationships/

The Proud Trust. (n.d.). *Find your local LGBT+ Youth Group*. https://www.theproudtrust.org/young-people/youth-groups/

TrevorSpace. (2020). *TrevorSpace - Community for LGBTQ young people*. https://www.trevorspace.org/

Very Well Mind. (2019). *Infatuation Is Fun, but Long-term Is Lovely Too*. https://www.verywellmind.com/what-is-romantic-love-2303236

Virginia Tech. (2010). *BIRTH CONTROL METHOD PERFECT USE (%) TYPICAL USE (%)*. https://healthcenter.vt.edu/content/dam/healthcenter_vt_edu/assets/docs/contra-fail-rate.pdf

Walden University. (n.d.). *10 Signs of a Healthy Relationship*. https://www.waldenu.edu/programs/psychology/resource/ten-signs-of-a-healthy-relationship

Weale, S. (2021, December 16). How to talk to your children about porn and other online harms. *The Guardian*. https://www.theguardian.com/society/2021/dec/16/how-talk-children-porn-other-online-harms

White, J. (2023, June 7). *735 Best Secret Crush Quotes To Express Your Feelings (2023)*. Clarity. https://www.consultclarity.org/post/secret-crush-quotes

Woods, A. Z. (2021, October 19). *75+ Quotes You Can Identify With When You Meet Someone Special*. Thinkaloud.net. https://thinkaloud.net/when-you-meet-someone-special/

World Health Organization. (2022, August 22). *Sexually transmitted infections (STIs)*. Who.int. https://www.who.int/news-room/fact-sheets/detail/sexually-transmitted-infections-(stis)

Zarrabi, R. (2022, May 16). *11 Huge First Date Red Flags | Psychology Today United Kingdom*. Psychology Today. https://www.psychologytoday.com/gb/blog/mindful-dating/202205/11-huge-first-date-red-flags

Made in the USA
Las Vegas, NV
04 May 2024